Condemned to Live

Frisch's unit used this bunker near the front in the Yelnya salient line near Smolensk, the scene of his most horrific fighting. Only the structure's name reminded them of home: "Wien (Vienna) 1941." Russia, fall 1941.

Condemned to Live

A Panzer Artilleryman's Five-Front War

By
Franz A. P. Frisch and
Wilbur D. Jones, Jr.

BURD STREET PRESS

Photo Credits: Franz A. P. Frisch except where otherwise noted.

Books by Wilbur D. Jones, Jr.
Condemned to Live: A Panzer Artilleryman's Five-Front War (Burd Street Press)
Gyrene: The World War II United States Marine (White Mane)
Giants in the Cornfield: The 27th Indiana Infantry (White Mane)
Arming the Eagle: A History of U.S. Weapons Acquisition Since 1775 (Department of Defense)
Congressional Involvement and Relations: A Guide for Department of Defense Acquisition Managers (DoD), Four Editions
From Packard to Perry: A Quarter Century of Service to the Defense Acquisition Community (DoD)
Glossary: Defense Acquisition Acronyms and Terms (DoD), Two Editions
Forget That You Have Been Hitler's Soldiers: A Youth's Service to the Third Reich (White Mane, 2000)

This Burd Street Press publication
was printed by
Beidel Printing House, Inc.
63 West Burd Street
Shippensburg, PA 17257-0152 USA

In respect for the scholarship contained herein, the acid-free paper used in this book meets the guidelines for permanence and durability of the Committee on Production Guidelines for Book Longevity of the Council on Library Resources.

For a complete list of available publications
please write
Burd Street Press
Division of White Mane Publishing Company, Inc.
P.O. Box 152
Shippensburg, PA 17257-0152 USA

Library of Congress Cataloging-in-Publication Data

PRINTED IN THE UNITED STATES OF AMERICA

Dedication

To the memory of the German common soldier of
World War II,
der Einfache Deutsche Soldat,
of whom I was one for nine long years

Contents

List of Illustrations viii

List of Maps xiii

Foreword xiv

Prologue xv

Preface.. xxii

Introduction xxx

Glossary xxxviii

Chapter 1   *Franz Frisch, der Einfache Deutsche Soldat*
                 Franz Frisch, the German Simple Soldier 1

Chapter 2   *Feldzug in Polen, 1939, und Frankreich, 1940*
                 Campaigns in Poland, 1939, and France, 1940 46

Chapter 3   *Feldzug in der Sowjetunion (Russland), 1941*
                 Campaign in the Soviet Union (Russia), 1941 69

Chapter 4   *Feldzug in Sizilien und Italien, 1942–45,*
                 und Kriegsgefangenschaft, 1945–47
                 Campaigns in Sicily and Italy, 1942–45,
                 and Prisoner of War, 1945–47 100

Chapter 5   *Ueber Kriegfuehren und zu Ueberleben Trachten*
                 On Waging War and Waging Survival 123

Chapter 6   *Franz Frisch, die Nachkriegsjahre*
                 Franz Frisch, the Post-War Years 145

Selected Bibliography 147

Index 150

Illustrations

Frisch's bunker on Yelnya salient line near Smolensk. Fall 1941 .... frontispiece

Horse and *panje* sled. Russia, fall-winter 1941 xvi

Frisch and battery mates study gun plans xvii

Artillery Regiment 109 ready to fire xviii

Kodak box camera similar to one used by Frisch on campaign xx

Frisch as a student before the war xx

Dr. Frisch at his desk, Defense Systems Management College
(present) xx

Frisch's battery moves into action. France, 1940 xxiii

Frisch at age twenty-four in 1943 xxv

Invading *Panzer* column moves on Sedan. France, May 1940 xxvi

Marcel's "Grand Garage" is no more. France, 1940 xxvii

Burning Russian structure. 1941 xxviv

Forward observer from Frisch's battery. Russia, 1941 xxix

OKH Order of Battle for the Battle of France. May–June 1940 xxxiv

Burned-out block of Polish town. September 1939 xxxv

Happy and triumphant infantry head for rest. France, June 1940 xxxvi

Destroyed Soviet armored car BA 40. 1941 xlii

French prisoners of war await processing xlii

Mail call in Artillery Regiment 109 in Poland. September 1939 xliii

10cm artillery piece made of snow, near Moscow. Russia, 1941 xliii

White birch trees from Poland become graveyard crosses for German
soldiers. Russia, 1941 2

Frisch with his mother, Margarete. Vienna, Austria, 1938 3

Frisch is the only survivor among these four artillerymen. France, 1940 4

Frisch's battery prepares to fire. France, 1940 6

Artillery field radio operator team. France, 1940 7

Artillerymen unload artillery shells. Poland, 1939 8

German troops exercise by playing games. France, 1940 9

German soldiers queue up for fresh canteen water. France, 1940 12

Artillery Regiment 109 vehicle insignia and license plate. Byelorussia,
   1941 12
Reliable Steyr staff car hauls members of Frisch's battery around
   Europe. Russia, 1941 13
The half-track *Krausmaffai* truck transports the regiment's heavy guns.
   Russia, 1941 14
Artillery Regiment 109's *Panzer* vehicle insignia. France, 1940 14
Frisch and comrades near Smolensk. Fall 1941 16
One of Frisch's officers addresses battery members. France, 1940 16
German infantry unit marches from the front near La Neuville aux Jogtes.
   France, May 1940 18
German officers inspect chateau as potential headquarters, near Paris.
   France, 1940 19
Comrade artillery soldier heads home on furlough. France, 1940 20
Frisch with comrades from same *Gymnasium* (high school) class in
   Vienna. France, 1940 21
Polish civilian refugees flee from combat areas. 1939 23
Type of NSU motorcycle ridden by Frisch and his battery's 10cm gun.
   Poland, September 1939 23
Comrades napping in Audi-Wanderer open staff car. Poland, 1939 25
Crude camouflage on bunker, Yelnya salient defensive line. Russia,
   September 1941 25
German intelligence party and sightseers survey destroyed Soviet T-34
   tank. 1941 26
Decapitated Soviet soldier. 1941 27
German troops on mess duty. Russia, 1941 28
Improvised showers. Soviet Union, 1941 31
Farm wagon transports wounded French soldiers along with refugees.
   1940 33
88mm Flak 18 gun pulled by half-track. Poland, 1939 34
Frisch's battery pauses during drive into Soviet Union to maintain
   Kanonen. 1941 36
Gefrierfleischorden, the "frozen meat medal," awarded to survivors of
   Winterschlacht im Osten, 1941–42, "the Winter Campaign in the
   East." 38
German field engineers ponder what to do with destroyed bridge.
   France, 1940 39
German armored car guards French captives in makeshift prison.
   1940 40
Retrieving telephone wire from forward observer posts. France, 1940 40
Frisch's column passes through one more French village. May 1940 42
Car carrying artillery crew tows twin anti-aircraft machine guns. France,
   1940 43
Debris of war on French battlefield. 1940 43

Disabled Soviet T-34/76 42 tank. 1941 44
Polish prisoners of war head toward the rear. September 1939 47
Destroyed Polish farm wagons and dead horses on the road to Posen.
    September 1939 48
Wehrmacht interrogates Polish prisoners. 1939 49
German staff car crosses temporary bridge built by *Pioniere*. Poland,
    1939 49
Polish women in the south of the country. October 1939 50
German infantrymen examine captured Polish artillery piece. 1939 50
Frisch stops for cigarette break in tent compound. Poland, 1939 52
German 10cm (nonmotorized) artillery piece accompanied by dispatch
    rider and horse. France, 1940 53
Panzer advance column halts in France. 1940 55
Germans examine destroyed French aircraft. 1940 55
Frisch and comrades unload supplies from truck. France, 1940 56
Bulletin board in French town announces name of saboteur
    condemned to death as warning to others. 1940 57
Frisch and companion with the communist driver of German staff car.
    France, 1940 57
"Hotel du October" gutted by fire. June 1940 58
French prisoners of war in temporary stockade. 1940 59
French poilu prisoners of war pass the advancing columns en route
    to temporary camps. 1940 61
French citizens flee the fighting. 1940 61
Panzers advance across France. Some days were faster than
    others. 1940 62
Occupation in France. Frisch's battery was quartered in this chateau
    near Rheims. 1940 62
Horch KFZ 15 staff car with equally popular Puch motorcycles.
    France, 1940 63
Wreckage of French city. 1940 64
Friends from Vienna with Frisch at lunch in Paris, 1940 64
German soldiers on leave near Eiffel Tower in Paris. France, 1940 65
Kapitaen and *Oberleutnant* of Frisch's battery with comrades
    at Rheims. France, 1940 65
Frisch's comrades tour Palace of Versailles near Paris. 1940 66
Frisch seated on Steyr staff car. France, 1940 67
Sign on hanged Russian partisan tells fellow citizens to beware of
    partisan activities. 1941 70
Soviet prisoners of war line up for head counting. 1941 71
Frisch's battery fires toward the front lines. Soviet Union, 1941 72
Downed Soviet Tupelov SB-2 twin-engine bomber. 1941 72
German soldiers examine an obsolete Soviet Polikarpov I 153 fighter.
    1941 73

Two comrades improvise shower-splash bath at stream in Russia.
Summer 1941 74
About to enter Smolensk. Russia, fall 1941 75
Frisch grabs some sleep in a Russian farmhouse. Fall 1941 76
Column halts outside a house in Russian village. Summer 1941 76
Sturmgeschuetz G III Aus E raises Byelorussian dust. 1941 77
Soviet fighter destroyed by German anti-aircraft fire. 1941 79
Flat Russian landscape and destroyed Russian bi-plane fighter.
Summer 1941 79
Committee of Russian peasants gathers to welcome Frisch's unit. 1941 80
Germans gather to view wreckage of Russian T-34/76 42 tank. 1941 81
Company street in Frisch's battery tent encampment. Soviet Union,
summer 1941 81
Frisch's battery rests with 10cm piece cradled in limber. Soviet Union,
1941 82
Taking time out for some water sports during the successful early
campaign. Soviet Union, 1941 88
Russian citizens knew how to dress for winter. 1941 89
German artillery trucks with broken springs or frozen engines.
Russia, winter 1941 90
Something less than the French chateaus: peasant farmhouses.
Russia, 1941 91
German soldiers make snowshoes out of rope coverings. Russia, 1941 92
In peasant farmhouse quarters, German soldier reads newspapers
from home. Russia, 1941 93
Friendly descendant of Czar Peter the Great, or Ivan the Terrible.
Russia, winter 1941 94
Soldier ventures down into shell crater. Russia, 1941 96
Frisch's battery *Kapitaen*. Russia, 1941 97
Frisch, sighting transit, during training in land measurement for artillery
spotting. Germany, 1942 101
Two new privates of 1st Battery who became Frisch's friends.
Italy, 1942 102
Kapitaen Mack musters 1st Battery, Artillery Battalion 557.
Sicily, 1943 105
Frisch comrade and mascot monkey. Sicily, 1943 106
Frisch with comrades at Poggio Berni. Italy, 1944 109
The French Maginot Line, built between the world wars to keep the
Germans out of France, bypassed by modern armored warfare
in 1940 111
Before the campaign in France. Frisch with young friend near Koeln.
Germany, January 1940 113
Artillery Regiment 109 conducts training session after fall of Poland.
1939 115

Direct hit on dirt road. Poland, 1939 116

"To Franz Frisch: From the History of the Automobile," for speech
    made at POW camp. Pisa, Italy, 1946 117

Frisch's column passes through damaged French city. Summer 1940 118

POW prayer book distributed by Vatican. 1946–47 119

West side of Maginot Line defenses between Germany and France.
    1940 124

City streets have been cleared of enough rubble to allow vehicle
    columns to pass. France, 1940 124

Infantrymen on bicycles pedal past Russian Orthodox church. 1941 126

The flat Russian terrain provided little protection for a German
    rifleman. 1941 127

German Mark II Panzer tank (PzKpfWII) heads for the front
    in France. 1940 128

Fresh snow-covered graves of Germans killed in the advance into
    the Soviet Union. Fall 1941 130

Announcement which got the Frenchman's attention:
    "Everybody who aids the English will be shot." 1940 131

Regiment's Christmas party. France, 1940 133

German soldiers examine downed French Potez 74.1 reconnaissance
    aircraft. France, 1940 134

Frisch and comrades enjoy rowing on lake in Loire Valley.
    France. Summer 1940 134

Christmas party caricatures spoof regimental life. France, 1940 135

Advancing columns pass disabled French heavy Char B1bis
    tank. 1940 137

German infantry proceed on bicycles. France, 1940 137

The local peasants were not afraid of their invaders. Russia, 1941 139

Overturned French's farmer's cart with fallen horses. 1940 140

Russian peasants gather for a burial. 1941 140

Signposts point the way to towns and German headquarters on the
    drive to Moscow. October 1941 141

World War I French soldiers' cemetery. 1940 142

Frisch and friends prepare to enjoy French café meal. Late 1940 143

Frisch with mother, Margarete. Circa 1948 146

Maps

Europe on the Eve of War, summer 1939 30
Invasion of Poland, September 1939 45
Invasion of France and the Lowlands, May–June 1940 54
Invasion of the Soviet Union, June–December 1941 68
Yelnya salient lines near Smolensk, Russia, fall 1941 83
Defense of Sicily, July 1943 99
German Defense of Southern Italy, September 1943 107

Foreword

I read this fascinating memoir from a unique perspective. Franz Frisch and I were both nineteen years old when we entered the army, Franz in the German *Heer* in 1938; I in the U.S. Army in 1942. Both of us "not long out of *Gymnasium*." Both artillerymen sworn to serve our country. Only fate and geography kept us from fighting each other. Franz served in Europe; I in the North Pacific. We met, became professional associates and friends at the Defense Systems Management College in 1987, and remain so to this day.

This book reflects the goodness, sensitivity, honesty, dedication and intellect I quickly learned to admire and respect in my friend and comrade. It was a poignant and touching read for me. He provides incredible insight of the life and culture of the German common soldier of World War II. He bares his soul when he describes the conditions, miseries, personal interactions, fears and dreams he experienced during his service. I found that to be startlingly—disturbingly—similar to my own thoughts as an American soldier in a different part of the world, but engaged in the same war.

As a soldier of thirty-five years and an amateur historian, I have nowhere seen anything to rival the candid photographs of the German soldier at the front or in camp. It is a marvelous and long-lasting contribution to the study of World War II. The insights of life on the Russian front in the winter of 1941 are unparalleled and unforgettable.

Edward Hirsch
Brigadier General, U.S. Army (Ret.)
Former Provost, Defense Systems Management College

Alexandria, Virginia
November 1999

Prologue

Finding Franz Frisch, the *Panzer* Soldier

The first snowfall of the winter came hurtling in sheets to the ground, but very little remained long where it fell. In the office coffee mess I poured my cup, glanced outside again, and headed down the hall. After a few steps I saw Franz, a distinctive professorial figure replete in customary tweed jacket, stopped with empty cup, leaning on his cane. He was staring pensively out the window at the snow, locked to some distant spot, and failed to notice me. "Franz, my friend," I said, *"Guten Morgen."* He did not reply. "Ah, the snow, you are looking at the snow," I continued. "This must remind you of your home in Austria—the winter sports—did you like the winter sports when you were young?" "No," he replied, never moving. Feeling drawn to his cogitation for a reason, not offended by this usually personable old man, I asked: "Well then, what does this remind you of?" A moment passed, and, still motionless and transfixed, he answered: "Russia, Russia."

Dr. Franz A. P. Frisch and I had been fellow faculty members at the Defense Systems Management College at Fort Belvoir, Virginia, since 1987. However, Franz, as low key as he is methodical, shared none of his background with colleagues. I knew only what the faculty biographical sketch book said about his vast experience in the shipbuilding industry and prestigious teaching positions. But at once, on that day in an early December, I realized there was so much more I wanted to learn about him.

As we talked in the ensuing weeks, I chanced raising certain questions, and, respecting my interest and feeling more comfortable, he began to open up. Yes, he had served in the German army in World War II, a matter he just had not discussed for many years. He was drafted in 1938 at age nineteen from his native Vienna after the *Anschluss,* and was discharged ultimately in 1947 after two years in an American prisoner-of-war camp in Italy—nine years of service to the *Wehrmacht*, and all the time but a private.

xv

During the fall–winter 1941, the Germans make the best of a Russian horse and *panje* sled for hauling their supplies across the frozen snow.

An artillery soldier, he fought in the invasions of Poland, France, and the Soviet Union, and in defense of Sicily and Italy. The latter two were against the United States. His was a five-front war, most unusual for a private of any branch of any army.

The Americans captured him two months before the war ended within a few miles of South Tirol. His weapon was a 10cm cannon towed by a half-track truck. He rode in a staff car. He was part of the *Panzers*, a motorized soldier, whose *Blitzkrieg* lightning assaults on the enemy forged the most overwhelming form of warfare ever seen, and propelled Germany into European domination.

That was Franz Frisch back then. But now, fifty or so years gone by, one would never imagine he had endured those horrific times. Charming, witty, and affable, slow cadence in speech purposefully offsetting a heavy accent, and in step unavoidable because of old infirmities, he commands attention and respect through his wisdom wherever he goes. As the quintessential teacher and sage, he remains *Panzer*-like to his countless numbers of students in the American and European defense establishments.

Franz built a reputation on post-war achievements, and from this modest man even those required much coaxing for him to divulge. Some years ago in Germany, he was a leader in the shipbuilding and shipyard

Frisch, *second from the left,* resting on arms, and battery mates study plans to their 10cm gun. The soldier seated second from the right wanted to be a priest, but died at Stalingrad. *Wehrmacht* enlisted men wore rank badges on the left sleeve. A red collar signified artillery.

Frisch, *seated, second from right*, with members of Artillery Regiment 109 in support positions ready to fire, near Minsk, USSR. Summer 1941.

industry who, like Dr. Wernher von Braun in rocketry and others, but a decade later, was invited to become an American. His industrial imprint soon extended through the U.S. Navy, American commercial shipyards, many foreign governments, and high levels of marine engineering academe.

As I studied my colleague, fascinating as his industry and academic achievements had been, I recognized his remembrances of war service simply had to be recorded for history and his family while his memory remained fertile. As a military historian and author, I asked if I could have the honor to write the story of his experiences, and he graciously consented.

My questions to him became more frequent and more direct, and to me, a serious student of World War II, more intriguing. *Yes, the snow, to the outskirts of Moscow in December 1941,* he said, wincing and muttering about the freezing cold. *We could see the streetcars.* With Guderian in France? *We chased them all the way to the Channel, then Hitler called us off.* Oh yes, Hitler. *He kept turning the screw slowly until all freedoms were gone. I saw him but once.* Then gradually coaxing became unnecessary, as I earned his confidence. The challenge then was mine to learn more about what to ask.

One day at the office, confiding in me after hours of interviews the previous week, he produced a nondescript tan envelope tied with string containing several hundred aging small photographs. They bulged out of packets marked in ink *Polen, Frankreich, Studenten-Jahre* and others, scenes of captured Polish, French, and Soviet soldiers crowded into make-shift compounds, dead crewmen on burned-out tanks, scarred pillboxes of the Maginot Line, a hanged Russian partisan, heavy cannons being placed into action, smiling comrades in knee-high jackboots enjoying French wine, rows of birch tree graveyard crosses, snow-bound German trucks, and his mother. Franz was in a number of them.

He had taken them, or had been a subject in them, on campaign with a Kodak box camera until he could obtain film no more, and his camera was lost. A frayed, marked-up wartime map of Italy dropped out, also a POW prayer book from the Vatican, and a 1946 handwritten list of men with Germanic names and addresses mostly in Austria. "Here, look at these things," he said. "I found them somewhere. I haven't seen them in fifteen or more years. Tell me later if you see anything we can use."

Anything we can use! You don't mean it! They themselves immediately became the focus of his story: pictures and items the likes of which I had never seen before. I was dumbfounded. Despite having a busy work schedule, I quickly shut my door and spent the next several hours looking at them, searching for Franz, straining to identify the subjects, then placing them gingerly back in their packets. They were our Rosetta stone. The story was now complete.

(A few weeks later, by sheer coincidence, I found an identical Kodak camera in an upstairs antique store in the Upper Peninsula of Michigan,

Kodak box camera similar to the one Frisch used on campaign. Gift of coauthor.
Photograph by Wilbur D. Jones, Jr.

Frisch as a student before the war.

Dr. Frisch at his desk, Defense Systems Management College (present).
Photograph by Richard Maddox, Defense Systems Management College

purchased it, and presented it to him. "Now you have your camera back, a souvenir, a gift." I recall well growing up in the war years and having a family Kodak of that type. They worked well for the common folk and common soldier.)

This special turn of events, these remarkable photographs and memorabilia, added a new dimension. We continued with fresh impetus to preserve his story, a rare glimpse into the life of the German common soldier of the war. I became absorbed with the *Panzer* artilleryman Franz Frisch of long ago, once my enemy. Excited, he responded appreciatively and enthusiastically as if a portion of the mind closed for many years, his own POW, had finally been freed.

Franz and I together proceeded to write his memoir, and soon an excerpted piece, primarily on his experiences in the 1941 campaign in the Soviet Union, was published in *World War II* magazine as the article "A Panzer Soldier's War." We titled his memoir *Condemned to Live*, based on a true contradiction in words expressing his frustration over chances for survival as the war turned against Germany.

Approximately the end of March 1943, I returned from convalescence leave to my unit, the 1st Battery of Artillery Battalion 557. The 1st Battery was all that was left from the unit 557 and was then located near the airport at Palermo, Sicily. The 2nd Battery made it to Tunis, North Africa, and after the landing went in best organized form into an American POW camp. And the 3rd Battery rests somewhere on the bottom of the Mediterranean after being torpedoed on the transport from Sicily to Tunis. Only the 1st Battery survived, and was again the core for a new 557, employed first in Sicily and then in Italy to the bitter end. I might consider myself very lucky to have missed assignment to the 2nd or 3rd Batteries, but instead I felt strongly from this time on my place in the German army was simply: condemned to die—condemned to live.

The *Panzer* artilleryman Frisch helped launch the European war in Poland, had a role in Germany's early military successes, endured some of its subsequent defeats, and continued his loyal soldierly duties until just weeks before his country surrendered. From this wide-ranging viewpoint, his memoir reflects an aspect of the war from the German side to which history has paid inadequate attention in English-language literature: the life, culture, and travails of the *Wehrmacht* common soldier.

Wilbur D. Jones, Jr.
Captain, U.S. Naval Reserve (Ret.)
Wilmington, North Carolina
November 1999

Preface

My recollections and photographs of World War II focus on people and how we lived and survived in the German army, the principal subjects being comrades and family. It is not meant to be a war history. To understand and enjoy the story, a reader need not be an expert on the European campaigns and battles, geography, *Wehrmacht* organization, or grounded in military history. I believe the book's introduction sufficiently contains such information to prepare the reader historically. My coauthor, Captain Wilbur Jones, and I have added a brief glossary, including the replicated translation of German terms we use, to facilitate the occasional transition to contemporary German words and terms.

My narrative is an extensive remembrance of experiences, reminiscences, and impressions in and out of combat. While drawing out my remembrances, I am compelled by circumstance of time and added wisdom to philosophize about the tragedy of Hitler, war and survival, and losing freedoms, the latter with ample warning to my fellow Americans. On these soul-searching thoughts, I ask the reader's indulgence.

Furthermore, the reader should keep in mind these remembrances are those of a private soldier, a *Soldat* or simple, common, soldier of the German army. (I later learned his counterpart was immortalized by American combat cartoonist Bill Mauldin as Willie and Joe, the typical "G.I. Joes" of the U.S. Army of World War II.) The narrative, therefore, conforms to the level of authority and responsibility, viewpoint, and informality of the man who took or posed for the images. Consequently, this work is only about those matters of concern, or brought to the attention of, *des Deutschen Soldaten* and the small and volatile world in which each of us alone and together struggled to exist.

The remembrances are from some twenty hours of taped interviews we shared, many extemporaneous conversations, and answers to written questions. Histories of the campaigns and modern maps were especially productive references. Jones extensively researched *Panzer* operations and each of my campaigns to corroborate the material and comprehend his environment. (The Introduction contains a chart showing the German

Frisch's battery in France, May 1940, with camouflaged 10cm gun moves into action behind the *Panzer* advance. The 10cm piece was called a "long distance" gun with a maximum range of twenty-one kilometers. He was then serving in the *Rechentrupp*, or calculation unit, which made corrections for commands to gun settings, one hundred yards behind the guns.

army order of battle for the invasion of France.) I jotted down notes which aided in the research, particularly when translating my artillery units' portions of the book by *Tessin, G, Vol. 6*, an official German government accounting of *Wehrmacht* units.

In focusing only on a social study of the common soldier, I avoided entanglement in Hitler's grand strategies, field marshals and generals, *Panzer* tactics, second-guessing victories or defeats, or recounting the history of the war. Such is way beyond the scope of this private's personal war.

Instead, I describe in text and photographs the soldier's life, including:

My background and why I wrote this memoir;

How I saw myself as a German common soldier: a wide range from the food we ate, to coping with the Nazis and the Americans, to furloughs at home;

How I waged war as an artilleryman, and survived the cold of Russia and the stupidity of some of my leaders; and

The campaigns I was so fortunate to take part in, and so happy to get out of—all told, you could say I somehow survived fighting on five different fronts.

Some people have told me my photographs of the European war are a significant contribution to the war's archives. Little did I ever expect that would be the case as I snapped pictures while campaigning in Poland, France, the Soviet Union, Sicily, and Italy. I shot pictures until 1943 when I could no longer obtain film. Not long after I lost my camera anyway. Periodically I sent the film home to Mother to be developed, and she held the prints for me.

The images display the devastation of the European war I have tried so hard to forget, but feel obligated to surface at this point in my life. They include battle action and the aftermath, dead soldiers, dead animals, destroyed towns, destroyed structures, and disabled war machines. Utter destruction all, so typical of that war—we created nothing but chaos and misery. I do have pictures of people, camp life, soldiers at leisure and recreation, the captured enemy, refugees, conquered citizens, comrades and friends, and my mother.

These photographs reflect my view from the field artilleryman's vantage point. My motorized unit usually was positioned in the third echelon of the advancing *Panzer* columns, which were spearheaded by armored units, tanks, and motorized infantry. (Coincidentally, about the time I began running short of film in 1943, my unit was no longer an attacking *Panzer* unit, but instead we were simply static-mobile defensive toys called to the nearest "hot spot." Being designated much earlier in the war as such a "fire engine battalion" certainly came true as we progressed ever backwards toward the Fatherland.)

When acting as an artillery forward observer, I frequently was in the front line, or ahead of it, an extremely dangerous position. My job was not to be a combat photographer. Consequently, the images are like the snapshots of a tourist (which often I felt I was), best friend, or team photographer—in the right place at the right moment. Most photos were taken during our "glorious advances" conquering other countries' possessions for the Third *Reich*.

Frisch at age twenty-four in 1943, a photograph sent to his mother in Vienna with a Mother's Day greeting.

With a jubilant private at the wheel, and a captain at his side, the invading *Panzer* column moves on Sedan. France, 1940.

Marcel's "Grand Garage" is no more, a victim of the German advance into France. 1940.

Except for showing a few hardships in Russia, and two German cemeteries, they are of the happiest and most confident of times. At least we were told so.

Do not be misled into thinking for a moment this was all there was to my war. Unfortunately I cannot show you the bloodshed and devastation imparted on our German forces, first of all because it simply was not opportune (remember that only victories were happening all around me until I got to the Mediterranean in 1943), plus there was some censorship, and the authorities frowned on anyone reporting negative news.

In this regard, I must emphatically state that I was totally unaware of how the Nazis were treating the Jews of Europe. I don't believe any of us common soldiers at the front or in training had any idea of the Holocaust. Only after I was captured did I hear any facts. The Holocaust, of course, was the war's most horrible outcome and its most reprehensible act. Never was my unit, or any unit with whom we were associated, involved in this matter to my knowledge.

I further ask the reader to put himself for a moment in the position of us German common soldiers, to hear and perhaps to empathize with how the war was affecting us at the time, and later in retrospect.

Franz A. P. Frisch, Ph.D.
Jackson, Mississippi
November 1999

Germans try to pull equipment from burning Russian structure. 1941.

A forward observer from Frisch's battery uses the upper level of a Soviet peasant's barn to spot artillery fire. Note the "U"-shape sight. Russia, 1941.

Introduction

The Land Campaigns in Europe

World War II began on September 1, 1939, when the German armed forces, the *Wehrmacht*, invaded next door neighbor Poland. It ended in Europe on May 8, 1945, when Germany surrendered to the Allies, her armies totally defeated on its eastern and western fronts, and much of her Fatherland destroyed or desolated. The most cataclysmic event in history, World War II, including the conflicts in Asia, the Pacific, Atlantic, Mediterranean, and other theaters, killed approximately sixty million people, military and civilians, and left countless millions wounded, missing, or uprooted and homeless. The human suffering was immeasurable, the national treasury of most participating nations drained or extended to the utmost.

To orient the reader about the European land war and its major events and organizations affecting Franz Frisch's involvement as German soldier, the authors provide a brief overview.

Adolf Hitler was directly responsible for World War II. An Austrian by birth but ardent German nationalist, he had joined the Nazi Party in the early 1920s. Once he took over the party leadership, the Nazi name would become the scourge of Europe and the world. Hitler's rise to power was born out of three compelling reasons: (1) Germany's quest to rebuild its economy after its collapse from the Treaty of Versailles, which culminated Germany's defeat in World War I, and in the Great Depression; (2) revenge for losing the war to its "natural" enemies, France and Britain; and (3) loathing of the communist Soviet Union. Hitler charmed the German people at the beginning by showing them a way out of their economic and national demise. The armed forces became the principal means of accomplishing his goals, and he devoted significant national attention and resources into rebuilding its numbers and stature.

On January 30, 1933, the opportunistic Hitler was appointed German chancellor by the aging *Reich* president and former army Field Marshal Paul von Hindenburg, having never been elected by the German people to any post. Fate played into Hitler's hands when Hindenburg died on

August 2, 1934. He forced the merging of the chancellorship and presidency, which gave him supreme command of the armed forces, and soldiers took an oath of allegiance to him personally. He then had a free hand as dictator, or *Fuehrer.*

Hitler intended to wage war to attain his objectives, and in 1936 ordered a plan for having the armed forces and the economy ready for war in four years. He believed war with Russia was inevitable, particularly to accommodate his long-standing dream of more *Lebensraum* (living space) for the German population. His first overt military act was to reoccupy in 1936 the Rhineland, the heavily industrialized western area of Germany taken away by the Allies after World War I. In March 1938, he took advantage of political unrest in Austria and annexed that country in the *Anschluss,* or joining up of his home country with the Third *Reich.* One year later, he sent troops into Czechoslovakia's Sudetenland, the German-leaning area across its border, and until 1918 part of Austria, to seize that territory. No one stopped him from these actions short of outcries and resolutions which he ignored. He was on his way to near total domination of the continent by 1942. Meanwhile, the scheming and relentless Hitler protected against Russian intervention on the east by signing a treaty with the Soviet Union, one he would tear up in June 1941 when the time came for him also to execute his long-term goal: conquering that nation.

Hitler staged an event on the Polish border used as a pretense for authorizing the immediate pre-planned attack on Poland on September 1. The *Wehrmacht* streaked into and across Poland employing a revolutionary type of warfare called *Blitzkrieg,* which utilized the *Panzers—tanks* and armored infantry—supported by attack aircraft and motorized artillery, to thrust fast and deep into enemy territory and surround isolated pockets of troops. By September 27, the first nation to surrender to Germany had fallen. Germany's principal antagonists, Britain and France, along with Australia and New Zealand, declared war on Germany two days after the invasion began. (Germany declared war on the United States on December 11, 1941.)

Europe then settled into the "Phoney War," while the world watched for Hitler's next move. On April 9, 1940, Hitler diverted attention from western Europe by attacking Denmark and Norway. Then on May 10, he launched the long-anticipated invasion of France, Luxembourg, Belgium, and the Netherlands. Five days later the Netherlands capitulated, and on the twenty-eighth, Belgium. *Panzers* reached the Calais coast and Dunkirk on the twenty-sixth, and despite having trapped hundreds of thousands of Allied troops on the English Channel beaches, were halted by Hitler, allowing most of them to escape to England. By June 14, Germans entered Paris, and on the twenty-fifth, a cease-fire ended the Battle of France. He was master of Europe.

Hitler's momentous decision to take his war to the Soviet Union precipitated the largest invasion of the war, and its bloodiest and fiercest prolonged campaign. Beginning on June 22, 1941, some 3.6 million German and other Axis soldiers (including Hungarians and Rumanians) with 3,600 tanks and more than 2,700 aircraft, crossed the border with the USSR through the partitioned Poland. For the opening weeks it was *Blitzkrieg* again at its finest. But soon the drive began to peter out because of over-extended logistics lines, command and communications problems, bad weather, and eventually the harsh Russian winter. In late November the *Panzers* reached the outskirts of Moscow, Hitler's strategic objective, but no further. Fierce Soviet counterattacks, and the extreme cold, for which the invaders had no winter clothing, combined to push the Germans back in December. In 1942 the Soviets gained the offensive and began forcing their enemy westward. German drives southward into Ukraine and the Caucasus ended in disaster at Stalingrad in February 1943 and at Kursk in July. From then on, the German advances turned into total retreat along the Eastern Front until the fall of Berlin in May 1945.

In 1942, as the Mediterranean war spread, German forces began augmenting Axis partner Italy in Sicily. British and American Allies landed in Sicily on July 10, 1943, and quickly swept aside the defenders, entering the objective Messina on August 17. With Sicily taken, the Germans and Italians escaped to the boot of Italy to prepare for the inevitable Allied landings. Italy surrendered on September 3. On September 9 the Allies came ashore at Salerno and Reggio Calabria. The arduous twenty-month campaign up the Italian peninsula, the Germans continuously on the defensive behind well-fortified positions, ended on May 2, 1945, in the northern Po River Valley. There the routed German forces, retreating hurriedly northward, surrendered.

Following the Allied landings in France at Normandy in June 1944, Paris was liberated on August 25, and the drive through France and Belgium toward Germany continued into November when a stalemate developed. In December, Hitler launched Germany's final massive assault of the war into the Ardennes Forest attempting to drive the Allies back to the Channel. It failed in the Battle of the Bulge, and the Allies capitalized by defeating the Siegfried Line inside the German border as 1945 began, and advanced on the Rhine River. The Americans first crossed the Rhine, Germany's last natural defensive barrier on the Western Front, at Remagen on March 7, and other crossings soon followed. By late March, the Allies were ready for their final campaign into central and southern Germany.

As the Americans pushed forward from the area of Mainz and Frankfurt, the Germans were reduced to uncoordinated and ill-prepared defensive efforts while retreating inward. Allied drives moved southward into Bavaria, Austria, and Czechoslovakia, until by late April few organized German units of size remained. In the meantime, the Soviets were rapidly moving westward and helped create a viselike grip on the enveloped enemy. On April 30 Hitler committed suicide in Berlin. Germany surrendered on May 8, called VE (Victory in Europe) Day, and the European war ended.

The *Wehrmacht*

In 1938, Hitler established the *Oberkommando der Wehrmacht* (*OKW*, *Wehrmacht* High Command) as the armed forces machinery for executing the coming war. He retained the title as Supreme Commander and named army Field Marshal Wilhelm Keitel as *Wehrmacht* chief of staff and army Field Marshal Alfred Jodl as chief of operations. Both remained for the duration of the war.

The *Wehrmacht* consisted of the three services, the army (*Heer*, the Army command was the *OKH*, *Oberkommando des Heeres*); Navy (*Kriegsmarine*); and air force (*Luftwaffe*), each seeking to preserve its vested interests. Each service commander had direct access to Hitler, making overall strategic coordination difficult. At their peaks, the army mustered 6.55 million men in 1943, the navy 801,000 in 1944, and the air force 1.0 million in 1942. The *Waffen-SS*, directed by the *SS* and only loosely associated with the *Wehrmacht*, surprisingly peaked at 830,000 in 1945. For the entire military, the peak was 9.48 million in 1943, twice its number when war began. *Wehrmacht* losses in killed in action were: army, 1,622,561; navy, 48,004; air force 138,596, for a total of 1,809,161. The total of men who died from other causes was 191,338. Wounded included: army, 4,145,863; navy, 25,259; air force, 216,579. The total missing was 1,902,704.

In 1939 the army consisted of the following number of divisions (total 106): six *Panzer*, four motorized (later *Panzer Grenadier*, or armored infantry), four light armored, 86 infantry, and a few others. By 1945, the principal division numbers had become (total 304, in varying degrees of strength): 31 *Panzer*, 13 motorized, 176 infantry, and 50 *Volksgrenadier*. True to Hitler's in-house policy of "divide and rule," to enhance his maintaining detailed direct control over the *Wehrmacht*, the air force had the parachute forces, some field divisions, a *Panzer* division, and the antiaircraft (*Flak*) forces. And of course there was the *SS* and *Waffen-SS*, which often operated without army control but in their areas. Conflicts arose over the chain of command. After June 1941, the Eastern Front became Germany's primary theater where sixty percent of the army forces were involved.

As the strong possibility of defeat faced Germany in 1944, Hitler in September created the *Volkssturm* (People's Home Defense Force) organization, making men ages sixteen to sixty (some younger, some older) liable for civil defense service at the home front. The *Volkssturm* did not fall under the *Wehrmacht* but was commanded by Heinrich Himmler, head of the *SS*. Because the men were also part of the labor force, training was accomplished on weekends. Arms and ammunition were scarce, and men

OKH Order of Battle for the Battle of France, May–June 1940
Army Group A (in Center between AG B, North, and AG C, South)

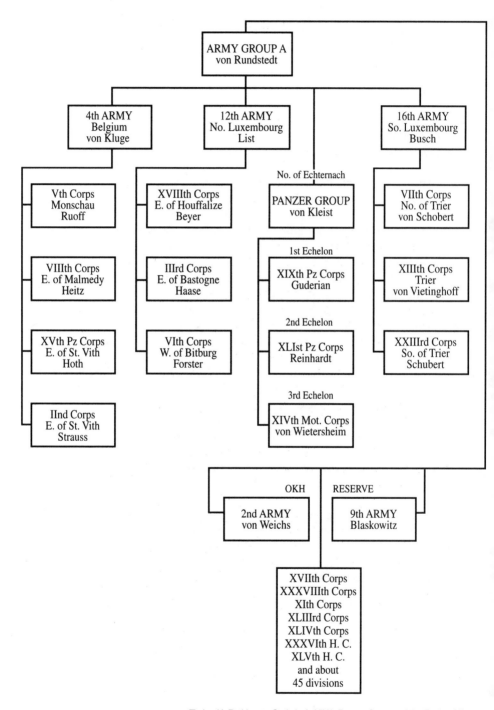

ARMY GROUP A
von Rundstedt

4th ARMY
Belgium
von Kluge

12th ARMY
No. Luxembourg
List

16th ARMY
So. Luxembourg
Busch

Vth Corps
Monschau
Ruoff

XVIIIth Corps
E. of Houffalize
Beyer

No. of Echternach

PANZER GROUP
von Kleist

VIIth Corps
No. of Trier
von Schobert

VIIIth Corps
E. of Malmedy
Heitz

IIIrd Corps
E. of Bastogne
Haase

1st Echelon

XIXth Pz Corps
Guderian

XIIIth Corps
Trier
von Vietinghoff

XVth Pz Corps
E. of St. Vith
Hoth

VIth Corps
W. of Bitburg
Forster

2nd Echelon

XLIst Pz Corps
Reinhardt

XXIIIrd Corps
So. of Trier
Schubert

IInd Corps
E. of St. Vith
Strauss

3rd Echelon

XIVth Mot. Corps
von Wietersheim

OKH   RESERVE

2nd ARMY
von Weichs

9th ARMY
Blaskowitz

XVIIth Corps
XXXVIIIth Corps
XIth Corps
XLIIIrd Corps
XLIVth Corps
XXXVIth H. C.
XLVth H. C.
and about
45 divisions

Florian K. Rothbrust, *Guderian's XIXth Panzer Corps and the Battle of France:
Breakthrough on the Ardennes, May 1940* (Westport, Conn.: Praeger, 1990), 131

The army passes through burned-out block of Polish town. September 1939. The "WH" on the license plate indicates vehicle belonged to *"Wehrmacht Heer,"* or army.

**Happy and triumphant German infantry head for rest in the rear in France.
June 1940.**

had to bring their own uniforms. By 1945, the *Volkssturm* was deployed
in the front lines, sometimes assimilating Hitler Youth groups to fight
alongside.

In the 1930s, inspired by General Heinz Guderian, the Germans
formed armored *(Panzer)* divisions for all phases of land warfare. Guderian
led *Panzer* forces into Poland, France, and Russia, and later was *OKH*
chief of staff. *Panzer* divisions ideally consisted of tanks, armored cars,
mechanized (motorized) infantry, motorized artillery, and motorized engineers. Deployment of these *Panzers* in *Blitzkrieg* attacks was the founda-
tion of Germany's army until 1943 when they lost the initiative (except for
the Ardennes offensive in December 1944), although most troops either
walked or utilized horses for transportation.

The accompanying order of battle for the invasion of France, May–
June 1940, is shown as an example of army field organization by *Panzer*
Groups, based on the OOB for Army Group A.

Franz Frisch's World of German Artillery

From 1938–1945, Private Franz A. P. Frisch was assigned to field
artillery units classified as nondivisional, or nonorganic (not dedicated on
the table of organization) to a particular armored or infantry division. Most
German artillery units in World War II were so classified as being part of a
general headquarters (generally from army through corps levels) force.

Headquarters made such units available to combat divisions for specific assignments primarily dictated by tactical requirements, such as invasions or other offensives, through detailing in the order of battle or temporary loan.

Frisch's field artillery units were classified as *Regimente* (regiments), or *Abteilung und Batterien* (detachments and batteries), and were mechanical: they were self-propelled,* and could be equipped with any caliber guns. His first unit, *Artillerie Regiment 109*, with whom he served until early December 1941 in Russia, was known as a "fire engine regiment," in a sense a mobile hired gun to be dispatched to various "hot spots": supporting *Panzer* units in trouble, bolstering a defensive line, or adding firepower to an attack. *Artillerie Regiment 109*, and also his subsequent unit, *Artillerie Abteilung 557*, which he joined in training in 1942,† were corps or pool assets. Such assets claimed no permanent home, and, as in the campaign in the Soviet Union, were sometimes shifted often enough to make his unit's frequent chains of command difficult for the common soldier to ascertain. (This problem clouded Frisch's memory in reconstructing to which organization he was assigned at a particular time.)

An armored *(Panzer)* division originally was assigned one regiment of two fully mechanized batteries of 24 guns (47 officers, 1,065 enlisted men), and later added a third battery of 15cm howitzers. Frisch's units were attached to *Panzer* divisions during the campaigns in Poland, France, and the Soviet Union, but, in keeping with the deteriorating tactical situations, were relegated to more static defensive elements in the Sicilian and Italian campaigns.

The army's field artillery weapons were standardized at calibers 10cm (or 10.5cm), 15cm, or 21cm, the former two classified as guns or cannons, and the latter two classified as "heavy" and howitzers. The *Abteilung und Batterien,* for example, could be equipped with any caliber gun. Weapons were designed to enhance production, maintenance, and supply by allowing a larger-caliber howitzer and a smaller gun to be interchangeable on the same carriage. *Krausmaffai* half-track trucks, and sometimes wheeled trucks, transported the guns and howitzers of Frisch's units.

The 10cm gun Frisch's units most frequently operated was the model *schwere* (heavy) *10cm Kanone* (cannon) *18 (*nomenclature *s 10cm K 18 [Bleiganz]).* The 15cm howitzers operated were the *15cm schwere Feldhaubitze* (field howitzer) *18 (15cm s FH 18 [Immergrun]),* the *15cm schwere Feldhaubitze 36 (15cm s FH 36),* and the *15cm Kanone 18 (15cm K 18).*

---

* The army moved most of its artillery and supplies with horses, contrary to a common misconception that *das Heer* was predominantly a modern mechanized force on wheels or tracks.

† Intended for *Afrika Korps* duty, his battery of *ArtAbt 557* never made it to Africa, but instead was deployed to defend Sicily.

Glossary

The following primarily German names, abbreviations, and terms are used in this memoir. German usage is italicized.

Abteilung Detachment; often used for a combined unit above company, but below regimental strength

Afrika Korps (Rommel's) Africa Corps

Anschluss Unification of Germany and Austria in March 1938

Artillerie Artillery

Autobahn Super highway

Barbarossa Code name for invasion of Soviet Union

Batterien Artillery batteries

Blitzkrieg "Lightning" war

Bundeskanzler Chancellor (of Austria or Germany), equivalent to prime minister; head of a government cabinet

das, der, die The

Deutsch(e) German(s)

Deutschland Germany

Diplom-Ingenieur Master of Science degree

Doktor der Technischen Wissenschaften (Doktor-Ingenieur) Doctor of Technical Science

Dorf Village

einfach Simple

Endsieg Final victory

Entlausungsstelle(n) Delousing station(s)

Feldkueche Field kitchen

Feldzug Campaign

Frankreich France

Frontbegradigung(en) Retrograde or readjustment of front line(s) (actually meant a retreat)

Frontschweine Front-line pigs (experienced troops)

Fuehrer Leader

Fusslappen Foot wrappings, foot rags (worn instead of socks in boots)

geborene nee

Gefrierfleischorden "Frozen Meat Medal"

Generaloberst Colonel general

Gestapo Secret State Police *(Geheime Staatpolizei)*

Grenadier Infantry unit

Gymnasium Approximate gross equivalent of large, extensive U.S. high school/junior college combination (academic emphasis on humanities, Latin, and Greek)

Haubitze Howitzer

Haus House, home

Hauswart Spy or informer within a unit

Heer Army

Heerestruppe Army troops (forces)

Heil Hail, greeting

Heimat Homeland

Heimaturlaub Furlough back home

Italien Italy

Jahr(e) Year(s)

Kanone Cannon

Kapitaen Captain

Kaserne Barracks, compound

Krausmaffei Company which manufactured a half-track vehicle

Krieg War

Kriegsgefangenschaft Captivity (prisoner of war)

Kriegsverdienstkreuz erster Klasse Meritorious War Service Cross First Class

Lebensraum Living space

Likoer Liqueur

Luftwaffe Air Force

Nachkriegs Postwar

Nazi Short for National Socialist German Workers Party *(Nationalsozialistische Deutsche Arbeiterpartei) NSDAP*

Oberleutnant   Lieutenant

OKH   Army High Command *(Oberkommando des Heeres)*

OKW   High Command of the Armed Forces *(Oberkommando der Wehrmacht)*

Panzer   Tank, armored

Panzergruppe   Panzer forces group, armored group

Pionier   Pioneer (engineer, reconnaissance unit)

Polen   Poland

Realgymnasium   See Gymnasium

Rechentrupp   Artillery plotting section (part of fire control)

Reich   Commonwealth; periods of German history: First *Reich*, Holy Roman Empire to 1806; Second *Reich*, Bismarck's reign, 1871–90; Third *(Dritte) Reich*: Hitler's "Thousand-Year *Reich*," 1933 to May 8, 1945

Reichsmarschall   Marshal of the Third *Reich* (Goering)

Regiment(e)   Regiment(s)

Ritterkreuz   Knight's Cross medal

Russland   Russia

SA   Storm trooper *(Sturmabteilung)*, "Brownshirts"

Scheisse   Shit

schuechtern   Shy, reserved, timid

Schwein(e)   Pig(s)

schwer   heavy

Sieg Heil!   Hail victory!

Sizilien   Sicily

SS   *Nazi* elite guard, protecting squad *(Schutzstaffel)*

Soldat(en)   Soldier(s)

Sowjetunion   Soviet Union

Spaet-Heimkehrer   Late homecomer

Steyr   Austrian company that built staff cars

Strasse(n)   Street(s)

Taifun   Typhoon, code name for Hitler's all-out assault on Moscow, 1941

trachten   waging, striving

Treffen   Reunion

Tornister   Knapsack, backpack

ueber   over

unser   our

Urlaub   Furlough, vacation

Vaterland   Fatherland, Germany

Volksgrenadier   People's grenadier unit

Waffen-SS   Military arm of the *Nazi* party

Wappen   Shield, crest

Wehrmacht   Armed Forces

Wehrmachtsbericht(e)   Armed Forces Report(s), selected military news
   brief(s)

Winterorden   Medal for winter service in Russia

Wunderwaffen   Miracle weapons

Wurst   Sausage

Road wreckage: a destroyed Soviet armored car BA 40. 1941.

French prisoners of war, mostly Moroccans, await processing in the rear of the action.

Mail call in Artillery Regiment 109 in Poland. September 1939.

Instead of making a snow man, what else would young artillerists of the German army make but a snow 10cm artillery piece? Near Moscow, 1941.

Chapter 1

Franz Frisch, der Einfache Deutsche Soldat
Franz Frisch, the German Simple Soldier

A scene I will never forget was in Poland, on the way home from the Russian front. It was the multitude of white birch trees and the crosses they made from them for dead German soldiers' graves.

I, Franz Adolph Paul Frisch, was born August 23, 1919, in Vienna, Austria. My father, Franz Xaver Frisch, a bank officer, died when I was ten. My mother, Margarete Frisch *geborene* Paradeiser, a high school teacher for more than forty years, raised me in Vienna.

On my father's side, he was a descendant of Hungarians active in banking and early industrial management. My father worked in banking according to his family tradition but was otherwise an ultra-liberal intellectual with the cynical humor of Werfel and other liberals of the Vienna circle of the post enlightenment. Nothing was safe from his wit and sarcasm except his deep commitment to family and his conscience. His father—so the story went—spoke not only fluent Hungarian (as well as German and French), but also Latin, classical Greek and Hebrew—the result of many years of education in a Jesuit seminary. After his time, the education level of the family rather deteriorated.

My mother was a descendant of an old line of impoverished Austrian aristocracy mixed with wealthy burghers. For generations they provided high government servants of absolute devotion to the Hapsburg crown, with inbred arrogance and complete lack of humor. She taught by choice mostly in the poorest districts of the city, and saw no contradiction between deep Christian religiosity, the ideals of Maria Suttner and Coudenhove Kalergi, and the humanistic aspirations of social democracy.

In my formative years, I grew up under what I thought was the fascinating auspices of the Christian-Austro Fascism of Chancellor Engelbert Dollfuss and Minister Kurt von Schuschnigg, and studied philosophy and political economy with eagerness. I took these studies far beyond the school's requirements. Out of more or less opportunistic reasons, I was to

The white birch trees of Poland became the graveyard crosses for many a young German soldier inside the Soviet Union. 1941.

make my hobby of that time, tinkering with technical toys, into my profession. My youthful dream of studying law as well as engineering and economics was only a partial success, at least as far as paper credentials were concerned.

Following completion of *Gymnasium* (high school) and the forced unification, *Anschluss*, of Austria with Germany, I was then "volunteered to participate" for seven years in the "Thousand Year Empire" of Adolf Hitler. My military service culminated in two seemingly unending years spent in an American prisoner of war camp in Italy. I returned home in 1947 to start my life over. Those nine years provided me with a unique opportunity for applied psychological studies in human behavior under stress, of winners and losers, about hopes and fears. While some of my comrades in arms considered our campaigns in Poland, France, the Soviet Union (Byelorussia and Russia), Sicily, and Italy either as a patriotic duty or a bore, I considered them an outstanding travel experience, the purpose of which was to study people, culture, and languages. This, I considered, was presumably the privilege of an outsider and nut such as myself.

Long before then I wanted to be an engineer. As long as the Austrian army existed, before unification, I wanted to be an army engineer officer. To be an engineer officer would have corresponded with family aspirations. My mother's brother tried to convince me that the only value of study was law, and that engineering was not sufficiently dignified. Engineering was always my interest and my aversion against law originated when they

Frisch wih his mother, Margarete. Vienna, Austria, 1938.

told me I must do it. As it was, I never counted with the German army and never counted with the war.

I was drafted into the army in 1938 at age nineteen along with many school and neighborhood friends. We entered service in the all-Viennese *Haus* (house) *Artillerie Regiment 109*. By tradition, this *Haus Regiment* belonged to the city of Vienna. I began as a private soldier, a simple soldier of the German army, and remained at that rank and servitude throughout my service.

Some forty-six years later, with reluctance and uneasiness, I agreed to tell the story of those nine years. I had never done this before, not even to my family. I had held my thoughts inside, those I had not purposely discarded. I am basically a bit *schuechtern*, or reserved. Perhaps it was the way my colleague, Wilbur Jones, whom I respected as a professor and historian, approached me that changed my mind. Then I did not know who might be interested in reading about my war experiences, but I realized this would be my only opportunity ever to speak for the record.

Hereafter follows some remembrances of those nine years of service to the *Wehrmacht* and some photographs to prove I was there. I would have taken more, but we simple soldiers could not get film after the summer of 1943. I was often diverted from sightseeing by calls to action, particularly as we were retreating, so I am almost without photos for Sicily and Italy, and

Frisch, *second from left*, is the only survivor among these four artillerymen. *On left*, Karl Koptik, who wanted to be a priest. France, 1940.

none for the American camp. Anyway, I lost the camera I used, an American Kodak box camera, and I had nearly forgotten what it looked like until Jones found one in an antique shop in Upper Michigan and gave it to me. I know that uncovering the photographs, which I had long ignored, made me more determined than ever to speak.

During my service, I kept no diary and later found no letters. But my memory remains clear in spite of reluctance to think of these things for so long. As evidence I found I repeated similar stories at different sittings during interviews. The photographs helped me remember, as did the questions of my inquisitor, Wilbur. He did remarkable in-depth research on my campaigns and those areas where I might have been so he could understand better what I was discussing. Translating my units' records from German forced me to recollect. I conclude these remembrances with a capsule of what little I have accomplished since 1947, the most notable being my fortune in settling in the United States.

I am glad this is all out in the open. I am much relieved of this "burden" of many years. I have always perceived a great reluctance on the part of soldiers of the "losing sides" to talk about what they went through. But now I wish to share it with my family, colleagues, historians, and other interested readers in hopes of providing them with a clearer picture of what life as a German soldier was like.

Let me say that first and foremost I fought only to survive. Of course, I also fought for my country as every good soldier must, but nothing was ever more important to me than survival.

The rank-and-file private simple soldier in the German army in World War II was called an *einfacher Soldat*, which was approximately the same as a "G.I. Joe" American common soldier.

For nine years, I always stayed a private. The main reason, I believed, was not my performance or my conduct, but that I had certain "political baggage" on the family side. Before army service, I was a member of the international boy scouts very much engaged with the Catholics, Fascism, and Chancellor Engelbert Dollfuss. The group I was associated with had pledged allegiance to the anti-*Nazi* Dollfuss. This for the *Nazis* was the same as being a communist in the United States at that time. Therefore, I entered the army with a bad political record, and I wasn't very eager to repair it, certainly not to give in to the *Nazi* interpretations.

To remain a private was almost preordained. Of course at the beginning I never thought service would take nine years of my life. I was thinking, okay, I have two years and then it's over, and then forget this shit. It certainly developed differently.

My family had served well in World War I for Austria. My father was a soldier before he got sick and was discharged. Both of my mother's brothers were officers. One was captured in Russia and was in a prison

Frisch's battery prepares for firing. France, 1940.

Artillery field radio operator team. Note rubber coat and rubber boot coverings. France, 1940.

camp in Vladivostok, and the other was on the Italian front. So I suppose it
was natural that I did my duty for my country.

Compared to the way I look today, army service actually changed me
physically very little. I am now 5-foot-6, about the same as in the war. I was
around 160 pounds during the war, not far from my weight today, although
placed differently. As a motorized soldier I always rode in a vehicle and
never marched anywhere. The exceptions were in 1942 after we were
withdrawn from the Russian front, when I marched during training in Czechoslovakia and in the closing weeks walking north before I was captured. I
was proud to be a motorized soldier. After the campaign in Poland every-
one talked about the overwhelming success of our *Blitzkrieg* attack, and I
figured it had to be our intense, detailed training as motorized soldiers
paying off.

Even though I entered the German army *(Heer)* with my hometown
friends in a homogeneous artillery unit, a characteristic that struck me soon
about the army was what we today would call its diversity. Starting with basic
training, a unit emphasized absolute geographic, social, and educational
mix. People recognized each other and sought to be at certain comfort
levels, and pretty soon you had subgroups which stayed together for so-
cializing, entertainment, and for various other reasons. There were certain
groups who visited the bordellos, and other groups who tried to stay away
and entertain themselves differently, reading, playing chess, and so forth.

The German army was a melting pot, if it can be called that, which
crossed the entire social and economic strata. We heard different dialects

Artillerymen's test of manual labor: unloading artillery shells in Poland. 1939.

German troops exercise by playing games. France, 1940.

but the more the unit got mixed, the more subsided the dialects. The advantage of this is the men learned to understand the different dialects and started to learn the true German language the first time, as my German friends would say, even us Austrians. Common German thus developed. When I was young you could drive fifty miles away and you almost couldn't understand the people. This in Germany and Austria is gone today completely. Vulgar and foul language was used probably about the same as in every army, but especially so when my unit was under heavy counterbattery fire in Russia and Italy.

At the beginning in 1938, our unit members were all Austrians. This is characteristic of a so-called *Haus*, or home, regiment. Every city had its own regiment. Vienna had a few *Haus* regiments, infantry, artillery, with only Viennese people. Germany had the same thing, such as Bavarian *Haus* regiments, etc. During the war my unit became more and more mixed with replacement soldiers. In the end no two *Haus* regiments were left in the German army.

Recruits, or draftees, were called into service in about September 1938. I entered *1. Batterie, 1. Abteilung, A. R. 109*, or 1st Battery, 1st Battalion, Artillery Regiment 109. We were located in the Vienna *Kaserne*, or compound, called the "Arsenal." The regiment's other two batteries were located in different buildings, and there was no communication among us. All three batteries were in Poland, France, and Russia from the beginning, and all three lost almost everything in the glorious 1941 winter offensive to conquer Moscow.

Whatever our title, my unit was never permanently assigned to another larger organization like a division. We were called *Heeres Artillerie*, or army artillery, and were shifted around periodically to a corps or division requiring immediate artillery help. We were never permanently assigned (the Americans would call such assignment system "dedicated" or "organic") like a fire engine being sent to fight a fire; or as we soldiers said, "where it stinks." Thus we were called the "fire engine battalion." Permanent reorganizations and unit name changes escaped the simple soldier, and ours had a number of them, but we remained essentially *Herrestruppe* on special assignments.

My artillery regiment, therefore, was a paper organization and seldom deployed as a complete unit, but rather as detachments. Consequently, as a lowly private taking orders from corporals and sergeants, I did not always know who were the generals above us; so it is difficult for me to reconstruct exactly alongside whom we were fighting or what commander we were attached to in many situations. I do recall a few division- and corps-level echelons we were assigned to for certain campaigns. One that sticks out most prominently was being with the 1st *Panzer* Division of (Major General Heinz) Guderian's Corps in the invasion of France, when we chased the Allies all the way to Dunkirk.

In reality, as I translated the event table in the source book *Tessin, G, Vol. 6*, the German government accounting of the *Wehrmacht* units, I thought how counter the organizational changes were to the myth of "German organization talent." For instance, to start a revolution in an organization, the revolutionaries must trust each other, and this takes time. If they are shifted around, no trust among them will exist, and no revolution will take place. Such an analogy would apply in our case, for whatever we were trying to accomplish, continuity of command and organization was definitely lacking. This uncertainty caused some confusion and mixed signals, and except for our immediate peers, who were prone to get along reasonably well together, did not enhance morale.

Our job was to provide artillery support for the *Panzers*, the tanks and armored and motorized infantry. Those two echelons advanced ahead of us. We were in the third echelon, sometimes on the front, most of the time a kilometer or two right behind it. Unlike most German field artillery units, which used horses to pull their weapons, ammunition, and support equipment, our guns and equipment were towed by trucks, usually the half-tracked *Krausmaffei*. We crew members in the battery rode in the trucks or in *Steyr* staff cars which had a convertible kind of top.

Most of the time the gun we used was the 10cm artillery *Kanone*, or cannon, with a maximum range of twenty-one kilometers. Sometimes we had the 15cm *Haubitze*, or howitzer, which could reach fifteen kilometers.[*] Both guns used the same chassis and the same tractor. For battery spirit, before the Russian campaign we devised a new identification symbol for our unit. It consisted of an Austrian *Wappen*, or crest, with a cross and the outline of Vienna's St. Stefan's Cathedral on it. We placed it on the rear of our vehicles to the right of the license plate.

My original battery contained approximately two hundred officers and enlisted men. Artillery Battalion 109—it was never a regiment; we had the title, but it was only a battalion—had all together eight hundred men. We were reconstituted (reformed and reinforced) in Brno, Czechoslovakia, after the first Russian winter, and received lots of new recruits for basic training, but with no guns. We troops from 109 were the only unit with field experience training there. After training, 109 was broken up into two parts. The group of 109 that I was with was assigned for transfer to the *Afrika Korps*, the other part back to the Russian front as a new unit. Very unfortunately, the unit going to Russia was butchered along with the Sixth Army at Stalingrad in 1942–43, and only a few men survived. After Stalingrad, something like approximately ninety-five thousand went into the Soviet prison camps, and I think only approximately four thousand came out. I lost many friends, and later considered myself extremely lucky to be in Sicily, waiting for the Americans' invasion we knew would come.

---

[*] The German 10cm field piece was equivalent to the Americans' 105mm howitzer, and the 15cm piece was similar to the 155mm howitzer.

German soldiers queue up for fresh canteen water. France, 1940.

The *Artillerie Regiment 109* created its own unit insignia, shown here to the right of the license plate. It is an Austrian *Wappen* (crest) with a cross and outline of Vienna's St. Stefan's Cathedral. Byelorussia, 1941.

The good old reliable Steyr staff car, with its own firewood. This car which hauled members of Frisch's battery around Europe was built in Steyr, Austria. Russia, 1941.

I adjusted quickly and easily to army life by learning the rules and even at a youthful age to keep eyes and ears open and mouth shut. I got along very well with my enlisted comrades. We seldom had time to go into local towns for recreation time, and ended up writing letters daily and drinking a lot. Beer and wine were usually available, especially in France, but not at all in Russia. As long as it was available, to those of us learning how to drink, if you are *never* completely sober, even a war can be fun.

The German army was very eager to establish entertainment centers, which in plain English are called whorehouses. I heard the American army wouldn't do things like this, not officially anyway. In the German army a man had to get a certificate for a prophylactic injection after exposure. He had to check into the medical office, which might deter some anxious boys. If somebody got sick or something, like with venereal disease, and did not have a certificate, he went to jail. If he had a certificate of course it was not his fault. There were rules and regulations for every conceivable situation, and we had to know them all and adhere to them.

Me? I just enjoyed the beer and wine and played a lot of chess. We had in our group a junior master chess player from somewhere in Yugoslavia. His German was not very good, but his chess game was fantastic. Slowly and surely we put together by coincidence a little group which permanently played chess, and in this group rank didn't matter. We just enjoyed the chess games.

The *Krausmaffai* half-track truck transports the heavy guns of Artillery Regiment 109. Russia, 1941.

The rear insignia appearing as a "T" is for Artillery Regiment 109. Panzer vehicles were marked with insignias designed by the units. Only one battallion existed in the regiment. France, 1940.

The relationships I had with my officers and noncommissioned officers were mostly careful and correct and depended upon their personalities. But overall, I was confident in them personally. I did not draw attention to myself or rock the boat, and thus avoided extremes one way or another. Discipline got more and more relaxed as the war went along, when we all lost some of our confidence. When it comes to military leadership, like everywhere, I found all types of people.

In Italy, once I was assigned as cartographer to the artillery battalion command post. There I made some good observations of our leaders. They included:

Type I: The *Activist*. Left every day early in the morning to "inspect" the batteries. Found everything okay because he forgot that the telephone announcing his visit was much faster than his car.

Type II: The *Big Mouth*. Never, *never* left his command post or bunker. Talked permanently on the phone with the battery commanders. Knew everything they wanted to tell him. Was a Human Zero.

Type III: The *Human Being*. A most marvelous man. Whenever the situation got serious, he showed up. Calmed the nerves down. Everybody trusted him and respected him. He got shot in an accident by a sentry in a rest area when he walked around during the night with his dog. He was a major from the *Afrika Korps* with the *Ritterkreuz* (Knight's Cross) medal.

I think all human characteristics like leadership, humanity, intelligence—not learned appearances—have a normal distribution, independent of rank, grade, and other attributes. In other words, no human being is perfect, neither on the positive or negative side; not all officers are geniuses, and not all enlisted soldiers are drones.

The health care in the German army—I say this now in retrospect—was pretty good. We had in every battalion one medical doctor plus sanitary personnel. If I felt bad I had no problem turning myself in for sick call and was not restrained. I never was real sick or on light duty. I maintained my health rather well. We tried to take care of ourselves as much as we could and aided each other. The health of the soldiers, except for hopeless situations such as the winter we were before Moscow, was mostly good in the German army. I would say our medical care was typical European, a Western style. The government provided soldiers with eyeglasses. I wore glasses and attached them by a band or wrap around my ears to hold them on, and carried a spare set in my pack. We had minimal eye and dental care.

Like many of my comrades, I smoked whenever I could get cigarettes. Privates could not obtain cigars, but some smoked pipes, although I never did. I didn't get the flu, only a bad cold from time to time, because I smoked too much. The only bad disease breakout happened in Russia in 1941 when most of us came down with diarrhea. There the local unsanitary conditions were a factor, and the quality and frequency of food we got

Frisch, *left*, with comrades. Near Smolensk, USSR. Fall 1941.

One of Frisch's officers, a reserve and judge in civilian life, addresses battery members. France, 1940.

at the front were questionable. The other time we faced that situation in extreme was when we began heading north of the Gothic Line in Italy.* Diarrhea couldn't care less about rank, intelligence, or attributes. I had it for a few days.

An example of health care was during the Russian campaign in December 1941, when I got frostbite in my right leg while driving a motorcycle during the retreat. My leg froze a little bit, not too much, but just enough to be recognized and requiring treatment. I turned myself into the hospital about three weeks before Christmas, and was not alone. So many thousands of German soldiers were incapacitated by frostbite and the cold. Medical personnel did the best they could and were happy not to be on the front lines. For me, the frostbite meant I was sent home to recuperate. In time, I knew I cheated the Russian winter, but it may have saved my life.

While at home recuperating, I got my first vacation to study one semester at the Technical University in Vienna. I was very lucky. It was a nice break even while recovering from that medical problem. It was my first time at the university where I ultimately got my degree, a very interesting and very beautiful but brief experience. At that time, the part of Artillery Regiment 109 I was assigned to was somewhere in Germany having returned from the front. A new unit was organized for the *Afrika Korps* and was being trained for African duty, and I was told to report to it after recovering.

Later, in Naples, Italy, in 1942, I got the jaundice and was sent home again to recover. I therefore attended my second semester at the university in the winter of 1942–43. After my leave I traveled by train and joined my new unit in Sicily.

German soldiers usually received home leave, or furloughs (vacations), once a year for two weeks. During campaigns we were not allowed to have furloughs. In 1942 I went home on leave twice, the second time for three months, and once again in February 1945 for two weeks to get married. The army paid for our way home and back, and we would ride the trains whenever possible. From France, we went between the campaigns in France and the Soviet Union. We were treated very well at home because everybody was in the same boat. (There was in no way discrimination, nothing like Vietnam when American soldiers returned home.)

The universities stayed open even though the student count was extremely low. Soldiers like me filled student seats temporarily and periodically. The professors, employees of the government, were mostly excused from military service, especially in the technical areas and in medicine. I don't know how it was in the humanistic area. Technical professors were allowed to stay and were a part of what we would call the "defense industry."

---

* In Russia, the supply lines were extremely long, especially as we got closer to Moscow, and once the snow fell, it was hard to get supplies into us. In Italy, our supply lines were always "north of us" and in our minds closer to Germany, and as we retreated northward more rapidly in late 1944 and early 1945, they moved ahead of us. Still, the German army was beginning to run short of means to supply its soldiers.

German infantry unit marches from the front near La Neuville aux Jogtes. France, May 1940.

German officers inspect a chateau near Paris as a potential headquarters. 1940.

The initiator of this "command to study" was—so the rumor went—*Reichsmarschall* Hermann Goering. He somehow determined that Germany would not have enough engineers and medical doctors after the great victory, the *Endsieg* (final victory, almost at hand!). Therefore, thanks to this strategic error in judgment, but fortunate error in my favor, he ordered that candidates with proven interests in those two disciplines should start their studies at government expense. I can also naively assume he did not know the truth—or refused to recognize its significance—from the front, like when the German army started, upon Hitler's order, the "last offensive of the war" in the winter 1941, with the goal to capture Moscow and end the war in the East, all before the snows would come.

On leave we soldiers had to have special permission to wear civilian clothes, so we did not have to run around in uniform. Otherwise we had to wear uniforms even at the university. At home, all were permitted to wear civilian clothes, but never wore civilian clothes on campaign. It was a privilege saved for vacations. Most soldiers tried to get rid of the uniforms on vacation to feel like normal human beings. This of course was impossible, as many men returned to cities suffering destruction from Allied bombing, although in my case, Vienna was not in bad shape. Other than serious rationing and other belt-tightening impositions, the Vienna city life was about as "normal" as one could expect during wartime.

After leave we either went back to our unit in the field or stayed at home. To return was what our orders stated and our sense of duty demanded.

Comrade artillery soldier at a train station in France headed home on *Urlaub*, or furlough. 1940. He died at Stalingrad in 1942.

Frisch, *left, seated*, with friends from same *Gymnasium* (high school) class in Vienna. Man on right wanted to be a priest; man seated second from right died in France; man seated to Frisch's left was captured at Stalingrad. France, 1940.

Any decision to stay home and try to hide meant that if we got caught, we were dead for certain. Men I knew, therefore, went back to our unit very carefully for survival. A German soldier went back to the front to fight simply because going forward gave him some sort of chance for survival. Going backwards (to Germany or Austria) was pretty certain the end of life. There was the old saying: You have to have more fear from your superior than from your enemy. The *SS* saw to it. The superiors were afraid to get shot, too, right up the line.

With the war obviously lost by February 1945, after my marriage I had trouble finding my unit in Northern Italy. They were closer to Austria than when I had left them. Some railroads were still running, but they were under frequent attack from aircraft. There was always confusion. Occasionally I found a truck, but I ended up on foot. I knew approximately where my unit was supposed to be, but communications were poor. Strange enough the army's organization started to break down in the rear. The closer I came to the front the better it was. I would have figured on the reverse situation. The organization at the front only broke down on purpose when General Heinrich Von Vietinghoff-Scheel and General Karl Wolff capitulated to the Americans in Switzerland in March.[*] Up to this point there was some nature of orderliness in the front lines, and I wish to pay tribute to the heart and courage of the German soldiers.

Like soldiers everywhere, we lived to get mail from home. We got mail fairly regularly, from home to front in two to three weeks. My girlfriend wrote me; my mother wrote me. To my knowledge, mail was not censored by the authorities except in the experience I relate later in this chapter. But we never knew, and the fear limited what we would say. We hesitated to bother people at home with details, bad as they were, because no one at home could do anything about it. The letters to us were mostly very short, very personal: we are healthy, don't worry about us, we love you, we pray for you. Mostly they tried to keep bad news away from us. We had a good idea what they were going through. Stories told by men who had been on leave were enough. In the German army there was a saying: *"Alles Scheisse, Deine Elli."* "Everything is shit, your *Elli.*" *Elli* was the name of the girl who wrote, *your* Elli, whatever her real name. For some reason I never collected or sent home any local or war souvenirs.[†]

---

[*] Vietinghoff, commander of Tenth Army, succeeded Field Marshal Albert Kesselring as commander in chief in Italy in March 1945. Along with Wolff, the Italian military governor and *SS* head in Italy, he immediately took over Kesselring's secret negotiations with Allen Dulles of the U.S. OSS (Office of Strategic Services) for a separate surrender of German forces in that country. The ultimate capitulation came six days before Germany surrendered. Kesselring was an outstanding soldier, and is remembered for his exceptional defense up the Italian peninsula that held down superior forces for twenty months.

[†] For Mother's Day 1943, I sent my mother a photograph adorned with a greeting. It is now framed and garnished with dried flowers. I displayed it in my former Virginia home.

Polish civilian refugees clog the roads, fleeing from combat areas. 1939.

The NSU motorcyle, from a famous German motorcycle manufacturer, the kind ridden by Frisch, with the 10cm gun used by his battery. Poland, September 1939.

Commanders at every level in the German army lived also with fear, fear of reprisal for failing to work miracles. Fear therefore drove the psychology of communications. Once upon a time, the messengers of bad tidings got beheaded. For our leaders, bad news was to be softened as much as possible: "This I cannot tell my boss." Hence, there was an improvement of any message from one level to the next in the command hierarchy, which I saw all the time in reporting combat conditions. After the war I read that this psychology was practiced by the men reporting to Hitler. Thus, a clear picture was difficult to get in many instances.[*]

Communications has its secrets and mysteries. Take one case in Russia. I never wrote bad news to my mother. She was a widow, lived alone, and the radio news from the front was, so I thought, enough for her. I prayed for her and tried to keep her spirit up. After about three weeks in the Yelnya (Jelna) defense area near Smolensk, I got a letter from her: "What happened at this particular time? I could not sleep and went almost crazy. And suddenly at such and such a time, I was again completely calm. What happened?" Turns out she missed the critical time in our withdrawal route from the Yelnya line by a single hour.

On what and how much we were told about the progress of the war, let me say that at my level we were never told what to expect. Only at the end did we know for sure what happened. Our incoming information was continuously controlled, and our outgoing was monitored and censored. The daily news we got was very questionable, even suspect. It was only "approved" news, regardless of whether by newspaper or radio. Everything was propaganda. The truth was hard to come by. The daily radio was the *Wehrmachtsbericht*, daily but filtered news from the front. This was selective to show the upside and sometimes it took a long time to get through. In the end the best news was when some of our radio operators could reach Allied news stations. We had enough people who understood sufficient English—I'm talking about in Italy—to listen to the news and get a few messages beyond what we heard on our own. I know that when we had a good radio at home, we made sure the door was closed, the shades were down, and the volume very very low as we were listening to the foreign news.[†]

Take the total disaster at Stalingrad, for example. I learned the truth about Stalingrad. During the time I had jaundice and received my second *Urlaub* in 1942. I followed the Stalingrad story, a massive German defeat, at home on the radio. It took a long time for the truth to come out. This was the end of "Do you want to talk of war?" Nobody at this time believed the

---

[*] In the chapter on the Russian campaign, I give an example of how battlefield communications were driven by fear (and some deceit) and consequently presented an entirely different view of what might be happening.

[†] "Black-listening" to Allied radio broadcasts by soldiers was widespread. [B. H. Liddell Hart, *The German Generals Talk* (New York: Quill, 1979) reprint, 293]

Comrades taking a nap in Poland in a Wanderer open staff car, of Wanderer-Audi manufacture. Audi had the front-wheel drive, Wanderer the rear wheel drive. It was used for telephone communication but not for gun crew transportation. Note the horse and wagon as the army's other means of transportation. 1939.

The artillery soldiers have placed some sort of crops or shrubs on top of their bunker as crude camouflage. Yelnya salient defensive line, east of Smolensk, September 1941. The counterbattery fire, particularly the Katuysha "Stalin organ" rockets, often was horrific.

German intelligence party and sightseers survey destroyed Soviet tank wreckage and the Soviet crewman who died trying to escape. 1941.

Decapitated Soviet soldier. 1941.

war was still winnable. After Stalingrad, no one with any intelligence believed that we could win the war. But hope was kept up by talking about the new *Wunderwaffen* (wonder weapons).

Religion was purely personal. I and others prayed privately but never openly. The opportunity to participate in religious services in the German army was relatively poor. We had services at Christmas and Easter, usually at no other times. At that time I was Catholic. (We attended the services even when they were of different faiths.) Many of the people who attended the services would be those with whom I could talk. It was, so to speak, an identifier. If somebody comes more or less regularly to Christmas and Easter you can slowly and surely begin to talk about politics. It was a kind of sign of trust. About 1940, the Nazis started to attack the Catholic Church for a short time. This led to passive resistance in many quarters. In the end, we go back to the old saying of soldiers, which was true in the German army: "There are no atheists in the trenches."

I got paid regularly and most of the money was transferred to my home address. We carried as many personal articles as we could hide. Officially we had a *Tornister*, carried on the back, as a knapsack. In our motorized unit we always had some space to carry a few private things, not many things, mostly books. We took writing paper but did not use stamps because postage was free. We always could find paper. On campaign we had toothpaste, a toothbrush, shaving cream, razor blades, soap—don't ask me about the quality. It was whatever came along. Today you wouldn't touch that kind of "quality." But we didn't have to buy them; they were our allotment. We fared pretty well. We also got a daily cigarette

German troops on mess duty prepare fresh-killed chickens for evening dinner. Russia, 1941.

ration. We always had a few friends who didn't smoke who would share theirs. For rolling tobacco into cigarettes we used mostly newspapers.

The quality of food in general, like the clothing and personal equipment (accouterments), was "bearable to sufficient." We had in Germany something called the *Feldkueche*, a field kitchen. Motorized units put the *Feldkueche* on a truck, but it was still the standard model of the *Feldkueche* that was developed at the time when we used horses to pull them. We had hot meals in Poland, France, and Italy. Food became cheaper and cheaper in quality. We had no prepared field rations like the U.S. Army's K-rations. We ate from the kitchen or foraged on our own—we always could find a chicken, except in Russia in the winter. I was never hungry enough to eat a horse. In Russia most soldiers carried a bag with potatoes and onions, even frozen. The food supply was often stopped because of impassable roads. The popular drink was coffee from the *Feldkueche*, or tea, frequently with rum. Soft drinks were unknown in the army. Our mess gear was the standard metal box with cover and knife, fork and spoon.

We were given only one set of uniforms, and didn't always get the uniform replenished while on campaign. The Russian campaign was a completely different story—we got nothing. We had no spare uniforms and had to clean our own uniforms and maintain them as best we could. In the cold weather, in both Russia and Italy, how could you remove your clothing to clean and dry it and try to stay warm? Blankets were hard to find, and after a while mere threads. When we were back in Germany or Czechoslovakia we always got new uniforms. We had three sets of underwear and one set of boots, which we wore until they wore out. These were replenished on campaign—it was absolutely necessary. Believe it or not, we in the artillery wore them out even though we didn't march. We weren't issued socks. We had *Fusslappen*, a piece of oversized handkerchief put around the feet, army issue, instead of socks. We wrapped it around the foot before putting it in the boot. My family sent socks, thank God, for *Fusslappen* and socks constantly wore out. Mothers are mothers regardless of the war or the army and will knit socks for their sons.

Regarding camp and personal hygiene and sanitation, when you are trained as a little child to keep yourself clean, to go to the toilet, to have a clean shirt, then you always try to do so. I think this holds true for all Western soldiers, regardless of whether German, American, or British. We tried to keep ourselves clean and our hair cut because we were used to it and recognized the obvious benefits from hygiene. Most units had a soldier who did barbering. We dug our latrines, and tried to wash ourselves when we could. In the artillery, we spent little time in trenches or foxholes, requiring us to relieve ourselves while remaining in them like the infantry. We did live in bunkers close behind the lines, and went outside to the latrines when we could. No matter how hard we tried, the sanitation situation became horrid if we stayed in one place long. The most difficult place, of course, was Russia

N. Ireland

Irish
Free
State

Great
Britain

London

English Channel

Belgium

Paris

Luxembourg

Rhineland

Bay of
Biscay

France

Switz-
erland

Spain

Madrid

Corsica

Mediterranean Sea

Sardinia

Norway

North Sea

Denmark

Netherlands

Sweden

Copenhagen

Memel

Baltic Sea

Berlin

Germany

Prague

Czechoslovakia

Vienna

Austria

Italy

Rome

Adriatic Sea

Yugoslavia

Belgrade

Albania

Estonia

Latvia

Lithuania

East
Prussia

Warsaw

Poland

USSR

Budapest

Hungary

Rumania

Bucharest

Bulgaria

Sophia

Black Sea

Greece

Sicily

Europe on the Eve
of War, Summer 1939

Germany Proper

German Acquisitions

0   100   200   300

Scale of Miles

The *Historical Atlas of World War II* (Henry Holt and Company);
Atlas for the Second World War (The West Point Military History Series);
Atlas of the Second World War (Geographia)

once our attack stalled. When we advanced in the early campaigns, we were in a hurry and whatever we did we left for those who followed. Sorry, but there was no alternative.

We used every possibility to bathe in some way, but sometimes all we had was for washing—a full bath—was a container of two liters of water. We were happy when we could do even this. It was easier to do in Poland and France, and sometimes Sicily and Italy, because of the weather and tempo of battle. Once in a while some men would bathe in streams or rivers. The general rule was: we tried to maintain a clean appearance even if contrived. This was more for sanitation purposes than for military requirements. We didn't really bathe in the winter, only sponged our hands and faces, sometimes our private parts.

At the beginning of the Soviet Union campaign, when the weather was good and the temperature warm, the soldiers improvised shower baths. 1941.

In Russia it was almost impossible to stay clean once the temperature began dropping. There, in order to stay warm, we took all the underwear we had and put it on, one on top of the other. In Russia we had a lot of lice, and we were practically helpless in fighting the lice. Everywhere a little bit behind the front there were cleaning stations where occasionally we got sprayed and had a shower bath to get rid of the lice. *Entlausungsstellen*, delousing organizations, they were called. We had to keep our uniform as clean as possible, especially during the winter. It was practically impossible to use proper hygiene to stay clean, and we smelled like it all the time. We improvised as much as possible, and as artillery soldiers probably didn't have it as bad as the infantry. We had no regular exercise periods because the war itself was exercise enough.

A spy of sorts was in every military unit. He was a political educator we called a *Hauswart*. The term *Hauswart* was taken from the organization at home, where every house had such a person as a political observer, mostly the janitor. In the army, he was mostly an old master sergeant. This didn't come about overnight. Slowly and surely this guy transformed from a *SA* uniform into a regular army uniform. The day before he had been unable to talk intelligently. Suddenly he was the representative of the *Nazi* party, and put political education into army companies. There were three rules: avoid him, if necessary be friendly, and keep your mouth shut. It worked for me.

I never encountered the *Gestapo*. Once we had to take over a position the *SS* had conquered, and we had to hold it. The *SS* had taken off. This was in the Yelnya defense line near Smolensk, and the Russians were beating the shit out of us. As for the *SS* reputation as good fighters, let's put it this way: The political indoctrination in the *SS* was obviously much, much stronger than in the army. The political indoctrination in the army, I would say, practically didn't exist. After the fall of France, in the Rheims coffee houses and restaurants the *SS* and army officers never mixed.

I well remember one instance of being indirectly involved with the *SS*. In May 1942, Artillery Regiment 109 was in Brno, Czechoslovakia training recruits. Then came the partisan attack in Prague, when the German High Commissioner in Czechoslovakia, *SS* General Reinhard Heydrich, was murdered. There was confusion in the compound and an immediate curfew for all soldiers. Next day, we experienced *Frontschweine*, or "front pigs"—battle-experienced troops—of the First Battalion were loaded onto trucks with our hand weapons. We were driven to the entrance of a small village to search for weapons of the partisans. We could hardly call it a village, *ein Dorf,* at all. It was really a collection of wine farmers in a valley stretched out over maybe ten miles. Vineyard-covered hills stretched along the middle and both sides of the valley. Farmers' houses were scattered along both sides of the road. Here and there, tunneled into the soft hills, were the farmers' wine cellars. We got the order to search the houses and wine cellars for weapons.

What an insane idea to send a bunch of combat veteran Viennese soldiers into wine cellars to search for weapons—in a Czechoslovakian village, where many Austrians, especially Viennese soldiers, had family origins in Czechoslovakia. The parody of an old Viennese folksong in dialect was: *"Mei Mutterl was a Wernerin, mei Fada war a Bem,"* and in high German: *"Meine Mutter war eine Wienerin, mein Vater ein Boehme"*...in English: "My mother was from Vienna but my father was from Bohemia." And besides, Austrians were not trustworthy anyway.

The farmers were not stupid. They invited us to test the wine. So we went from house to house and wine cellar to wine cellar in order to search for weapons, in reality to test the wine. A few hours later all of us were most happy and drunk. We would not even recognize a gun if we had found one. A *SS* unit was coming along behind us. Local people tried to keep our men inside their houses so the *SS* would leave the Czechs alone. It would have been an offense by the *SS* to check a house that had already been checked by the army. Thus we marched back to the trucks and the search was ended, and we received our deserved and definitely needed rest.

Farm wagon hauls wounded French soldiers along with refugees. 1940.

An 88mm Flak (primarily anti-aircraft) 18 gun, with splinter shield, pulled by a half-track. In Poland it was used not against air but against land targets. Frisch's battery had one, but it was for experimental purposes. Some of Frisch's regiment's guns were destroyed or damaged: "The other side had ammunition too." 1939.

The overall subject of morale, looking back, is difficult to gauge. I was in so many places, on so many fronts, under such differing circumstances. There were certain things we tried not to talk about. We couldn't say "they" were idiots and didn't know what "they" were doing. But most of all, we had to have a positive attitude. If you didn't have a positive attitude you kept your mouth shut in order not to get into trouble, which is something I learned quickly to do anyway.

For example, in Italy in 1945 we had to keep going north. There was no alternative except to surrender, and we all knew the Allies had insisted on "unconditional surrender." The idea that something was going bad for the German cause was clear to everybody after Stalingrad. I don't know whether anybody really believed it could be reversed. I doubt it. The American soldier was in a completely different situation. I think the American soldier had an idea that he could win the war. He may have had an ideal or goal to win the war, but on the German side since Stalingrad, survival was the only goal of the individual soldier and the unit—no other goal than survival. On the Italian front against the Americans the desired situation to come into was where we could capitulate. In Russia it was a different story. In Russia it was only if you couldn't move any more.* By the way, I never knew of a German soldier deserting. For God's sake, where would he go?

My unit and I were never engaged in close-up combat. I never saw a live enemy soldier face-to-face, except prisoners of war. Miraculously I was never wounded. I don't have any idea why not; everybody else was, it seems—and I was personally shot at only when serving as a forward observer, ahead of or equal to the front lines, and often in an extremely vulnerable position with very high casualty rates. Everything missed me but stirred up dirt and rock around me. I carried the standard-issue Mauser infantry rifle all the time and in Italy also a P-38 pistol. The equipment I used and operated, including the cannons, was of high quality and reliability. The exception was the trucks which I discuss in the chapter on the Russian campaign.

Besides being a forward observer and on the calculating team, I served as a telephone wire layer and motorcycle messenger. As an artillery soldier, I am asked about its effect on my hearing. First, earplugs were unknown in the German army. We tried to cover our ears as best we could. I don't know whether my current hearing problem is traceable to the gunfire or not, but I certainly listened to enough cannon fire that it is likely.

My unit received no medal or award but I myself did, like every *Soldat* on the Russian front in the winter of 1941–42. It was *Winterorden* and the

---

* Hart quotes the chief of staff of Fourth Army (of Army Group Center) before Moscow about the desire of the soldiers to press on. "The troops themselves were less depressed than their generals. They could see the flashes of the A.A. guns over Moscow at night, and it fired their imagination—the city seemed so near. They also felt that they would find shelter there from the bitter weather." Motivation enough, it would seem, for us. "But the commanders felt that they were not strong enough to push those last forty miles." [Hart, *op.cit.*, 185]

Frisch's battery pauses during drive into Soviet Union to maintain 10cm *Kanonen.* 1941.

Kriegsverdienstkreuz, the lowest rank of war service medal, and in soldiers' slang what we called the "frozen meat medal," or *Gefrierfleischorden*. It was given to all men who survived the first winter there, but the medal was soon lost after the war. Thanks to my colleague in writing this memoir, who must have visited many flea markets to find it (and that Kodak box camera), I now possess the long-lost "frozen meat medal" again.

I could never bring myself to the point of hating the enemy. Strange, but I understood them better than I understood myself. At the war's end, I felt one hundred percent positive about the Americans. The Germans and Austrians then looked at them as some kind of liberators. They were to me, even though they would detain me for two years in a prisoner of war camp. There was absolutely no animosity between the American soldier and the German soldier. I'm saying soldiers. The American political units, the people who came over after the war, had a completely different attitude. They had not fought the war, but they overplayed their roles as victors over the vanquished. The American soldiers we fought showed a mutual respect from soldier to soldier. Perhaps it had something to do with common basic Western cultures, morals, and religions.

I tried to be a good soldier and survive and avoid problems. Let's put it this way: In late 1939, early in my army life, I had an experience when we got transferred from Poland to the area of Bonn, Germany. We were at a military training base and suddenly we got the order we could only write open letters. Ah, censorship. I wrote a letter: "Dear mother, I have the honor to write you an open letter because it seems they don't trust the word of a German soldier." This caused me some trouble. Then I learned to keep my mouth closed.

Mother had warned me sufficiently, and I should have known better. It was back in March 1938 and the German troops came to take over Austria. It was when Hitler "unified" the two countries, the *Anschluss*. We watched. She told me, "Franz, please keep your big mouth shut. If you don't do it for yourself, do it for me." I then became paranoid about attacks on freedom.

I saw Hitler once, in his triumphant march into Vienna after the unification, and his oratory in front of the Hapsburg Palace. My feelings about the *Nazis* were all negative. The German army, caught in the middle, tended toward opportunism, but was never dedicated to Hitler. The army overall, and we soldiers individually, always tried to stay at arm's length from *Nazi* organizations and political units and the *SS* in particular.

I must comment briefly on Hitler's rule. Today an American might say the German generals had no guts to stand up to Hitler. But there is something missing, something Americans simply cannot understand. Nobody can understand who wasn't living through this absolute dictatorship where you were forced to make a decision between truth and your life. This is something I tell people when I talk about Europe in the classroom. Hitler

The *Gefrierfleischorden* ("frozen meat medal") awarded to Frisch
and other German survivors of (reverse side) *Winterschlacht im
Osten, 1941–42,* "The Winter Campaign in the East." Coauthor
found and presented this authentic duplicate to Frisch, who had
lost his original.

Photograph by Wilbur D. Jones, Jr.

German field engineers ponder what to do with this destroyed bridge: rebuild, repair, or go around? France, 1940.

German armored car guards French captives in makeshift prison compound. 1940.

Retrieving telephone wire from forward observer posts. France, 1940.

wasn't an idiot. He was crazy, but not an idiot. He did not start by shooting people. In the beginning, for example, let's assume there was a manager of a large factory who was against the *Nazis.* Hitler didn't shoot this guy. Instead he promoted him to general manager of a chicken farm on the North Pole. Who wants to be a general manager of a chicken farm on the North Pole? His replacement surely wasn't interested in the same and quickly got the message. This gradual increasing pressure turned the screw slowly and surely—nobody at the time realized it until it was too late. This exists in no book; there is no analysis. All the world talks about is the atrocities, where they can make a photo, and statistics about the millions.

Frisch's column passes through a nameless French village main street. May 1940.

Car carrying artillery crew tows twin anti-aircraft machine guns. France, 1940.

Debris of war on French battlefield includes French and German helmets, boots, uniform fragments, machine gun, and trash. 1940.

Disabled Soviet T-34/76 42 tank. 1941.

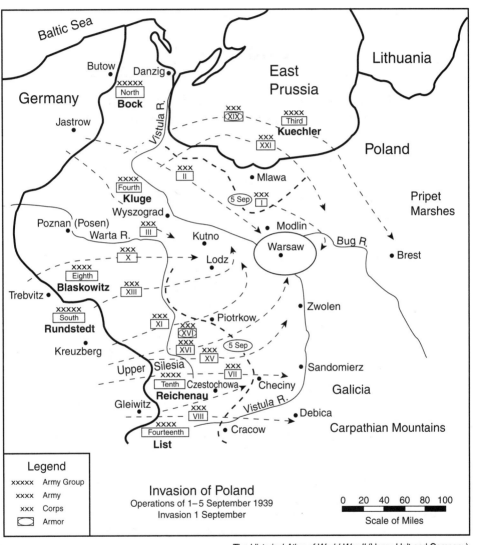

Baltic Sea

Butow
Danzig

Germany

Jastrow

Lithuania

East
Prussia

Poland

XXXXX
North
Bock

Vistula R.

XXX
XIX

XXXX
Third
Kuechler

XXX
XXI

XXXX
Fourth
Kluge
Wyszograd

Poznan (Posen)
Warta R.

XXX
II

Mlawa

5 Sep XXX
I

Modlin

Pripet
Marshes

XXX
III

Kutno

Warsaw

Bug R.

Brest

XXX
X

Lodz

XXXX
Eighth
Blaskowitz

Trebvitz

XXX
XIII

XXXXX
South
Rundstedt

Kreuzberg

XXX
XI

Zwolen

Piotrkow

XXX
XVI

XXX
XVI

5 Sep

XXX
XV

Upper Silesia

Gleiwitz

XXXX
Tenth
Reichenau

Czestochowa

XXX
VII

Checiny

Sandomierz

Galicia

Vistula R.

XXX
VIII

Debica

XXXX
Fourteenth
List

Cracow

Carpathian Mountains

Legend

xxxxx Army Group
xxxx   Army
xxx   Corps
⬭   Armor

Invasion of Poland
Operations of 1–5 September 1939
Invasion 1 September

0   20   40   60   80   100

Scale of Miles

The Historical Atlas of World War II (Henry Holt and Company);
Atlas for the Second World War (The West Point Military History Series);
Atlas of the Second World War (Geographia); *Blitzkrieg* (Time-Life Books)

Chapter 2

Feldzug in Polen, 1939, und Frankreich, 1940
Campaigns in Poland, 1939, and France, 1940

Pictures of France I still see: dead people, burning houses, dead horses. These are not very pleasant memories. I tell you, there is no difference between the smell of a dead horse and a dead human.

Poland, September 1939

I had been a German soldier in training for more than one year when we came to realize that we in the *Wehrmacht* were destined to be human tools of Hitler's political policies and lust for world power.* My unit, Artillery Regiment 109, was with the Fourth Army, XIX *Panzer* Corps when it invaded Poland from Germany in the northwest. Our goal was not Warsaw but rather it was toward Czestochowa. The date was September 1, 1939, and as we know it actually started World War II. I was doing what I had been trained and equipped to do, to back the armored forces and motorized infantry with field artillery support.

We were well supplied with food, ammunition, clothing, and essential supplies, and were blessed with good weather and little resistance. My battery was permanently engaged in action and fired many rounds toward the enemy, supporting the army's advances. Our assault was led by tanks and motorized infantry and quickly termed *Blitzkrieg* (lightning war). It was swift and sure, and the Polish armed forces were soon overwhelmed. Poland surrendered on the twenty-seventh, a short four weeks later. The success of our first battle certainly impressed us, and casualties in my unit were nil. Later, looking back, after the problems of Russia and Italy, I could not believe how easy it really was.

---

* Hitler's goals centered around expansion of German living space, *Lebensraum*, which were unattainable "without invading other countries or attacking other people's possessions....Further successes are impossible without the shedding of blood." Poland, his easterly neighbor, was the target for his first blood, and my first war. [Hitler quoted in numerous sources]

Polish prisoners head toward the rear. September 1939.

Several campaign remembrances stick out in my mind. Although the weather was clear and aided in our advance, the Polish heat was punishing and dust was thick.* At times we were very thirsty, even though we rode in vehicles, because we failed to stop long enough to adequately replenish our water supplies and gave much of it to thirsty infantry foot soldiers we passed. We encountered thousands of Polish refugees trying to flee from us to the East. Sometimes their numbers clogged roads and they had to be moved so we could pass. Some had been killed by aircraft, perhaps our own artillery. Otherwise, the Polish people didn't obstruct or stand in our way. In the utter confusion, fright, and panic, they just ignored us and kept away from us. I also remember we learned the words to the song *Lili Marlene,* never to be forgotten by any German soldier.

Within a couple of days my unit entered Posen and we were in the center of a *Kaserne* (camp, barracks). Over the radio we heard about the British-French ultimatum to Germany, announced over the loudspeaker. Suddenly nobody spoke. You could hear a needle drop. At that time I think everybody suddenly had the feeling that this was the end. Now we are going to be in a big war. Britain and France will come to Poland's aid. At first the morale was lifted through the success in Poland, which nobody had expected, but when we heard about the ultimatum from France and Great Britain, it dawned on a lot of people, myself included, that a catastrophe was developing. You saw that picture there, all those guns and

---

* Early fall was usually a rainy season in Poland, an element which normally would retard a *Panzer* advance. However, the roads and fields remained dry and hard and could facilitate men and machines. Luck was with the invader.

Destroyed Polish farm wagons and dead horses clutter the road to Posen. September 1939.

Wehrmacht interrogates Polish prisoners of war. 1939.

German staff car crossing a temporary bridge raised by army engineer battalion, the *Pioniere*. Poland, 1939.

Polish women in the south of the country, after the campaign concluded. October 1939.

German infantrymen examine captured Polish artillery piece. 1939.

trucks, everything beautiful, stationed in order, and over the loudspeaker came the announcement of the ultimatum.* What mixed emotions we had. It was one of the two most significant experiences I will always remember. The other was the reconnaissance-in-force I discuss in the chapter on the Russian campaign.

Another picture I will never forget happened at the end of the campaign in Poland. We were in a big meadow, in front of us a little hill, and suddenly a girl came down and was dancing, like in a ballet. My friends and I only looked at her, and then she disappeared. It was almost mystical. There I was sitting, happy that the battle was more or less over, and then suddenly a girl came out on a hill and was dancing a ballet. I haven't the vaguest idea what the background is, but I still see it. I don't know whether it was real or my imagination—I only remember that I saw it. This must have been another omen to us: the illusion of victory, tempered by the practicality of a future of more reality.

France, 1940

After some weeks in Poland, the shortest and most decisive campaign I was on, my unit was sent to Czechoslovakia for training in the Carpathian Mountains, and later in the spring of 1940 to western Germany on the borders with Luxembourg and France to prepare for the invasion of France and the Low Countries. This was the period after the British and French had declared war on Germany. It was called the "Phoney War," when combat had ceased, and the only action we heard about was the hurling of epithets and propaganda across the lines at French soldiers. We were stationed behind the German *Westwall*, or Siegfried Line. All we did was train and watch the worst weather Europe had seen in years halt all plans for the invasion, which Hitler kept postponing. My unit, like others, was left on edge, so to speak. We anticipated much, but we were not sure exactly what.

In final preparations for the invasion we were near Cologne and then the Eifel mountain region occupied by Army Group A (center group) under General (Gerd) von Rundstedt. On May 10, we began advancing southwestward through Luxembourg and Belgium on our way into France. France was the army's objective, but with the massed German forces not every unit could attack directly into that country. We bypassed the French Maginot Line defense far to the north and would not see it until many weeks later after we had finished our campaign and it had been immobilized.†

---

* Later we learned that Soviet armies also had invaded Poland from the East, and that advancing unalerted German and Soviet forces had met by chance, with some casualties, around the Bug River in central Poland. It was an unwelcome omen.

† Rundstedt commanded forty-six divisions, including seven armored and three motorized infantry divisions. The advance went partially through the Ardennes. The little opposition was primarily French cavalry. The German plan called for the *Panzers* of Army Group A to head south, then turn for the English Channel to force Allied armies into entrapment in Belgium. The plan mostly worked.

Amid tent compound in Poland, Frisch stops for cigarette break. *Panzer* artillerymen slept four to a tent. 1939.

Das Heer used many horses, too. German 10cm (nonmotorized) artillery piece moves forward accompanied by dispatch rider and horse. Note World War I French victory statue in center. France, 1940.

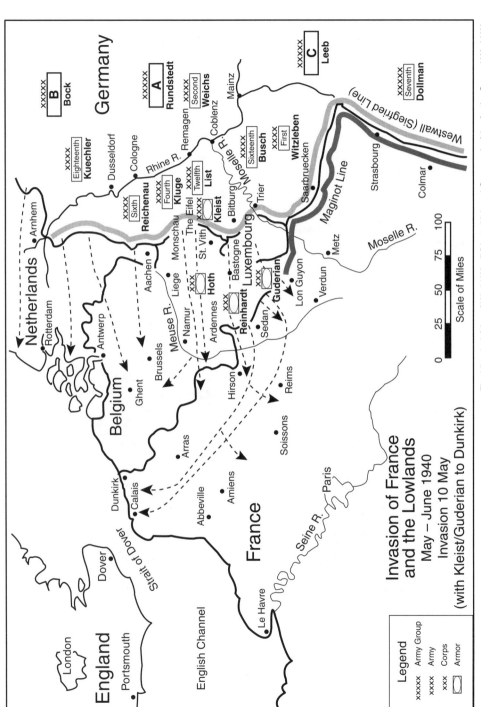

Invasion of France
and the Lowlands
May – June 1940
Invasion 10 May
(with Kleist/Guderian to Dunkirk)

Legend
xxxxx Army Group
xxxx Army
xxx Corps
◊ Armor

Scale of Miles
0   25   50   75   100

The Historical Atlas of World War II (Henry Holt and Company): Atlas for the Second World War

Panzer advance column halts in France. *Sturmgeschuetz* G. III is tracked vehicle, *front left*. 1940.

Germans examine destroyed French aircraft. 1940.

Frisch, *center*, and comrades unload supplies from truck. France, 1940.

This time we fought under General Heinz Guderian, the famous *Panzer* leader who had developed the armored and motorized warfare philosophy and had practiced it in Poland.To the best of my recollection, for most of the time my regiment was attached to (Field Marshal Wilhelm) List's Twelfth Army, (Colonel General Ewald von) Kleist's *Panzer* Group, Guderian's *Panzer* Corps, and Kirchner's 1st *Panzer* Division.

We headed south past Bastogne for Sedan and Rheims, making remarkable time but facing stiff resistance from French troops. We flanked the Maginot Line far to our left and arrived at Sedan approximately May 13. After taking Sedan, my regiment remained with Kirchner and headed west, then northwest, leaving Paris miles to our south, and turning toward the English Channel. Kirchner's objective was Montreuil S.M. on the Calais coast. We proceeded through the areas of Montcornet and St. Quentin.

My unit acted as *Heeres Artillerie*, or a floating army artillery regiment, not belonging permanently to any particular division or corps, but in all cases being assigned to someone's command. Still assigned to Kirchner, we reached the Calais area approximately May 21, exceptional speed since May 10. Along the way ultimately to Dunkirk we encountered only French troops, no British. We saw a few enemy aircraft but they had no effect on us.

My regiment got all the way to the outskirts of Dunkirk around Gravelines, where we, along with thousands of German tanks, infantry vehicles, artillery pieces, and soldiers, literally stopped in our tracks. On May

A bulletin posted on a wall in a French town: "The mechanic Marcel Brossier was living but because he sabotaged telephone cables he has been condemned to death and shot." Such bulletins served as a warning to others. 1940.

Frisch, *right,* and companion share wine with the driver of the Steyr staff car, a German army soldier (a communist), whose dress depicts his political feelings toward the war. France, 1940.

Somewhere in France on the drive to the English Channel, fighting gutted the "Hotel du October." June 1940.

24, Hitler ordered a halt for all German forces, and allowed the British and other Allied forces there to escape by water to England. My unit never actually got to the Channel or Dunkirk, but we got to within artillery shooting distance. Later we learned that more than 300,000 Allied troops escaped to England. Why we didn't go on in and take them we couldn't figure out, but it was one of the foremost questions I can remember arising during my time in service. I believed the German soldier could not care less about destroying them. Life was much easier whom nobody did any shooting, and we figured the French and British were through anyway. Later we understood that was what *Der Fuehrer* said. To even a simple private, it appeared to be poor military judgment and was a matter of regret four years later when the enemy gave it back to us many times over.[*] Two days later Hitler allowed us to take Dunkirk, by then of little value.

---

[*] Guderian in his book *Panzer Leader* [New York: Ballantine Books, 1957; 97–98] recites the order he gave to his Army Corps on May 26. Its reading in the field I remember. Most of it reads, "For seventeen days we have been fighting in Belgium and France. We have covered a good 400 miles since crossing the German border: we have reached the Channel coast and the Atlantic Ocean. On the way here you have thrust through the Belgian fortifications, forced a passage of the Meuse, broken the Maginot Line extension in the memorable Battle of Sedan, captured the important heights at Stonne and then, without halt, fought your way through St. Quentin and Peronne to the lower Somme at Amiens and Abbeville. You have set the crown of your achievements by the capture of the Channel Coast and of the sea fortresses at Boulonge and Calais. I asked you to go without sleep for 48 hours. You have gone for 17 days. I compelled you to accept risks to your flanks and rear. You never faltered. With masterly self-confidence and believing in the fulfillment of your mission, you carried out every order with devotion...."

French soldiers in prisoner of war temporary stockade, during the advance to Dunkirk, 1940.

After the push toward Dunkirk we got reassigned in eastern France as part of the occupation and went down to the Loire Valley near Nevers, and ultimately were stationed at Rheims. At Nevers we were close to the demarcation line which divided the country into occupied and unoccupied (Vichy) halves. We heard that Paris was taken on June 14, and wondered with some excitement if we would get to see the city. The campaign was continuing, but we were not part of it. (France surrendered on June 22.)

France was beautiful at that time, and the wine was fantastic. I remember well the food and wine, the sect, the *Likoer* we found in the houses in France. We had feasts and got drunk. In fact, every day we got a little bit drunk. But I also practiced speaking my French. The German propaganda told us we had to go to France in order to feed the poor French population; they were starving. We were living in French houses and there was so much food we couldn't eat any more. We knew the propaganda was bullshit. A few months later I visited the Maginot Line as a tourist. We were well supplied with everything we needed.

I did not encounter any French women during the campaign. In fact, the only French citizens we saw were refugees. When life started to be normal, that aspect of the occupation was different, and I can say I enjoyed France and some of the French. My unit stayed for about a half year in France in a little village near Rheims. Every weekend with a few trucks we went into Rheims, a beautiful place, very cultivated, and we had more or less the freedom to enjoy life. It was a good break for us. I visited Paris several times. I was most impressed by the cafés and wine and the Eiffel Tower, wondering if it had anything to do with the German mountains of the same name where we had assembled our large force for launching the invasion.*

The German high command *(OKW)* formulated the idea of a German invasion of Great Britain, and we started to get instructions about how to handle the guns and equipment in order to get there, but this "pipe dream" faded.† Eventually, in early 1941, we were transferred direct to Poland to train for yet another invasion. This time it was to be of the Soviet Union, where we quickly got, let's say, mentally cold feet, then in six more months literally cold feet. In the terrible months to come, we young men would remember the pleasant times in France, which surely was the most stress-free period of my army life.

---

* Since then, I have had no desire to return to Paris, and haven't.

† Operation Sea Lion, debated within the high circles, was scratched by Hitler.

French poilu prisoners of war pass the advancing columns en route to temporary camps. They were allowed to carry belongings. 1940.

French citizens flee the fighting. 1940.

As the *Panzers* advanced across France, some days were faster than others—the same in any army. "Hurry up and wait is a normal military operation," Frisch recalls. 1940.

During the occupation of France in 1940, Frisch's battery was quartered for a while in this chateau near Rheims.

The Horch KFZ 15 staff car with the equally popular Puch motorcycles, made in Steyr, Austria. *"WH"* on the license plates stood for *Wehrmacht Heer*, or German army. "T" on fender means towed artillery. France, 1940.

Wreckage of French city as Frisch's unit closely followed the *Panzer* attacking forces. 1940.

Friends from Vienna, Walter Fallmann and Gustav Penold, with Frisch, *center*, at lunch in Paris, 1940.

German soldiers on leave near the Eiffel Tower, Paris, 1940. Sacre Coeur church is in the center background. For Frisch, the visit to Paris was "too fast." He never went back to Paris after the war. "I don't know if Paris ever made too much of an impression on me."

A *Kapitaen* and *Oberleutnant* of Frisch's battery at Rheims, France, with some of his comrades. 1940.

Frisch's comrades tour Palace of Versailles, near Paris. 1940.

Frisch seated on Steyr staff car. Note side markings: "1/A.R. 109," "*Erste Batterie, Artillerie Regiment 109.*" France, 1940.

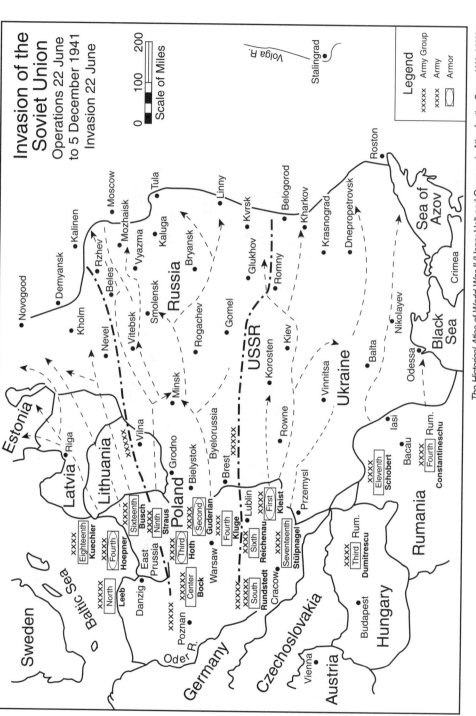

Invasion of the Soviet Union

Operations 22 June
to 5 December 1941

Invasion 22 June

Scale of Miles

0   100   200

Legend

xxxxx Army Group
xxxx   Army
⬭   Armor

The Historical Atlas of World War II (Henry Holt and Company): Atlas for the Second World War

Sweden

Baltic Sea

Estonia

Latvia • Riga

Lithuania

Vilna

Poland

Grodno

Bielystok

Brest

xxxxx
Eighteenth
Kuechler

xxxx
Fourth
Hoepner

xxxxx
Sixteenth
Busch

xxxx
Ninth
Straus

xxxx
Second
Guderian

xxxx
Third
Hoth

xxxx
Fourth
Kluge

xxxx
Sixth
Reichenau

xxxx
First
Kleist

xxxx
North
Leeb

xxxxx
Center
Bock

xxxxx
South
Rundstedt

xxxx
Seventeenth
Stülpnagel

xxxx
Eleventh
Schobert

Danzig

East
Prussia

Poznan

Oder R.

Germany

Warsaw

Lublin

Cracow

Przemysl

Byelorussia

Minsk

Nevel

Vitebsk

Smolensk

Rogachev

Gomel

Kiev

Korosten

Rowne

Vinnitsa

Ukraine

Balta

Odessa

Black
Sea

Nikolayev

Crimea

Sea of
Azov

Rostov

Kharkov

Krasnograd

Dnepropetrovsk

Belogorod

Romny

Glukhov

Kvrsk

Linny

Bryansk

Kaluga

Vyazma

Mozhaisk

Moscow

Kalinen

Rzhev

Beles

Kholm

Demyansk

Novogoed

Russia

USSR

Volga R.

Stalingrad

Czechoslovakia

Vienna

Austria

Budapest

Hungary

Iasi

Bacau

Constantineschu

xxxx
Fourth Rum.

xxxx
Third Rum.
Dumitrescu

Rumania

Chapter 3

Feldzug in der Sowjetunion (Russland), 1941
Campaign in the Soviet Union (Russia), 1941

It snowed from a certain time on in October. Snow was permanent, and if I was in those flat areas I could hear the snow blowing day and night. Never stopped. It drove me nuts and crazy.

After France, in late 1940, we transferred to Poland near the Bug River to prepare for the Russian campaign. The General Staff would call it Operation *Barbarossa*, but to the simple soldier the prospect was not so inviting, and thus we were told nothing specific. This withholding of information from the rank and file had become the custom, for what purpose I never could understand, for it kept us in the dark and did nothing to inspire us to work harder for the *Vaterland* (Fatherland).

The attack began in the early morning, about 3:00 a.m., on June 22, 1941, with an extremely heavy bombardment before the *Panzer* assault. Our unit was part of the bombardment—the "drumfire"—from firing positions along the front. The sustained heavy fire caused an incredibly uncomfortable level of noise. I remember, too, the night was very short, only several hours.* There was at the time a demarcation line between Soviet and German partitions of Poland. The invasion actually started from the area of the Bug River near Brest-Litovsk into the eastern part of Poland occupied by Russians, rather than directly into the Soviet Union itself. We later successfully entered the Soviet Union through Byelorussia.†

---

* That night is the shortest of the year in northern Russia, known as "white nights," because the sun never sets. The Germans opened fire with approximately six thousand guns. In the surprise attack, the Germans captured all essential bridges along the five-hundred-mile Bug River front.

† The strategy for *Barbarossa* gambled on shattering the Soviet resistance in a few battles of encirclement. Some units penetrated about 270 miles the first week, and confidence soared. After only five weeks, however, the Germans had begun to flounder in the vastness of Soviet space, and a continual front line could not be kept.

69

The hanged man with sign draped around him tells his fellow citizens the perils of being a Russian partisan against the Germans. 1941.

Soviet prisoners of war line up for head counting. 1941.

Frisch's battery fires toward the front lines. 1941.

Downed Soviet Tupelov SB-2 twin-engine bomber. 1941.

German soldiers examine an obsolete Soviet Polikarpov I 153 fighter. 1941.

In this campaign my unit designation remained as Artillery Regiment 109. We were in the middle section of the invasion forces with Field Marshal (Fedor von) Bock's Army Group Center. My unit was still being employed like a "fire department" and were assigned as needed, usually to heavy action, of course. Consequently this is what makes it sometimes difficult to reconstruct my unit's exact command structure or location on every campaign or battle. We began the attack assigned to Field Marshal (Gunter Hans von) Kluge's Fourth Army, and later we were with General (Hermann) Hoth's 3rd *Panzer* Group at Smolensk and General (Erich) Hoeppner's 4th *Panzer* Group before Moscow.

I know we did report up the line to some famous *Panzer* commanders in various campaigns like Guderian of the 2nd *Panzer* Group, (General Erich) Hoeppner, and Hoth. We frequently ran into Guderian. We soldiers called him by the nickname "Hurrying Heinz." This reminds me of the large letter "G" painted on all his *Panzer* vehicles for pride and unit identification. *Panzer* division leaders placed their initial on the rear of their tanks and vehicles.*

We crossed the Bug north of Brest Litovsk, which of course was within pre-war Poland, and advanced eastward. We were in the battles along the Yelnya Line near Minsk, the Minsk to Smolensk supply route, the battles in the woods of Orsha and Baratino and near Bryansk, and the one at Smolensk.

---

* Army Group Center began with fifty-one divisions, nine of them *Panzers*.

The fighting around Smolensk in July and August was the heaviest and deadliest I saw during the war. Russian soldiers captured at Smolensk paraded past us to the rear. They were much more distasteful and shabbier looking than any we had ever seen on the Western front. I recall seeing Field Marshal Kluge near Smolensk giving orders, what for I didn't know, but he was the highest-ranking officer I ever saw in the field. For us "little soldiers" the appearance of such high officials was without meaning, for we had not much of an idea what we would be up to next. I also recall seeing with amusement several signs raised by *Panzer* tank troops along the roads leading from Smolensk that read, "To Moscow."*

In the area of Smolensk (about 350 miles into the attack) in the Yelnya-Desna River salient, we began our first orderly retreat around September 1. Officially it was called a "planned withdrawal," and a "correction of the front lines." In the propaganda news perhaps the sweet expression, "correction of

Two comrades improvise shower-splash bath at stream in Russia. Note tan on man on left. Summer 1941.

* Minsk, about two hundred miles inside the USSR, fell to Hoth on June 26, Smolensk in mid-July, with some 138,000 prisoners. Toward the end of August the Soviets had lost 700,000 casualties and one million captured, and had surrendered their country's five hundred westernmost miles. German commanders were confident the drive should continue on to take Moscow, but Hitler disagreed and directed many of the *Panzer* forces southward in late July to assist in taking the Ukraine. The decision cost us invaders in the Center front dearly in time, manpower, and equipment.

About to enter Soviet city of Smolensk. Fall 1941.

the front lines, was proclaimed as a victory."* I presume so. But to me it was so much bullshit. The Russians were kicking us badly, and we had to regroup. By the first snowfall in October, we tightened the Yelnya lines again, and took another step backward.

Sometimes we would go in front of the infantry as forward observers. I didn't like that because we were shot at, and all we had to shoot back with was small arms. How long we went as observers always depended on the situation. Sometimes we sat in forward observer positions maybe one to two weeks. Now with this kind of situation started an army communications problem. When we talked with our commander in the rear our communication was very simple. We just started the situation off with a single word, *"Scheisse,"* or "shit"—bad—which it usually was, and went on from there. There was an unofficial twisted way of reporting the situation up the line. If the situation was bad, you reported, "shit." That means the situation was very bad. Now he to his boss cannot say that it is very bad; so he says it is "serious." And so on to the next level he "has it under control." Then when it is finally reported to the top it has become a "victory." This was my first practical course in army command communications and the cultivation

---

* The term is *Frontbegradigungen*, a retrograde or adjustment to the lines. Here the Germans were stretched too thin with no resiliency (under-strength divisions were assigned to cover indefensible twenty-mile fronts, with no reserves or replacements available). Around Yelnya, a salient extended some fifteen miles, inviting the inevitable Soviet counterattack.

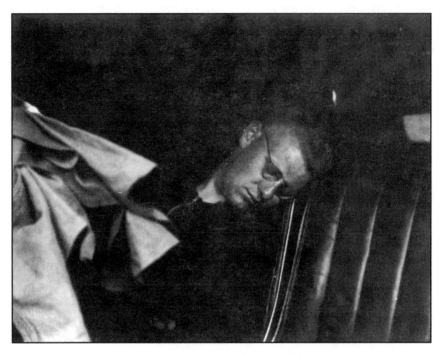

Frisch grabs some sleep in a Russian farmhouse. Fall 1941.

The column halts outside a Russian village house in the summer, before the rains and mud came. Note the construction of logs and straw. 1941.

Sturmgeschuetz G III Aus E raises Byelorussian dust. 1941.

of feedback up the hierarchy. We soldiers were powerless to change it or stop it. Who were we, and what were we to know?

The next day—or maybe a few days later—we heard on the radio, in the "news from the front" *(Wehrmachtsbericht)* about the "successful front correction" in our Yelnya defensive line, which was east of Smolensk, and the enormous losses we had inflicted on the enemy. But no single word was heard about a retreat, about the hopelessness of the situation, about the mental and emotional stagnation and numbness of the German soldiers. In short, it was again a "victory." But we on the front line were running back like the rabbits in front of the fox. This metamorphosis of the truth from "all shit" to "it was a victory" baffled me, and those of my comrades who dared to think. It took me roughly twenty-five years to understand this ugly phenomenon, when I started to study the psychology of communications and also the biological limitation to communicate.

The records of my unit indicate some success of our artillery in stopping the enemy attacks around Yelnya. That is definitely interesting. However, we "little soldiers" did not know how successful we had been. Such is the nature of and lack or precision of artillery fire. You do not always realize whether you have hit your target, or whether some firing randomly has caused casualties or structural and equipment damage. Sometimes the forward observer can report back that you have hit this or that. But the art of artillery is indiscriminate, to be sure. If you advance, you might be able to draw some measure of your success or lack of it. If you retreat, all you realize is that the enemy keeps coming at you, no matter what you give him to stay away. We definitely would find this out later near Moscow.

I well remember the retreat from the Yelnya line. We had nearly exhausted our supplies of artillery ammunition, and did not provide the proper counterbattery support of infantry. As such our battery received a constant amount of Soviet artillery fire, and casualties, which was meant to show we were unwelcome there.

I remember we did not receive a resupply of shells until days later when the front settled. It was pitch dark and we tried to make it back to the main front line. Every truck, every tractor with its gun, every soldier was on his own. I believe some infantry units covered the retreat. I was driving a motorcycle with a sidecar, a 600ccm NSU machine. But nobody knew where the battery commander was, and I guess he did not know where his guns were. Happily or unhappily, he participated in the retreat like any little soldier—without organization, without communication, and without command. This was perhaps the most vicious battle I remember of the entire war, even Cassino.

Our forces recovered, held the lines, and continued the advance. In the fall of 1941, our regiment was divided and some were sent to reenforce the drive by Army Group South on the Ukraine. I remained with the unit in Army Group Center. I don't remember whether we all got back together for the final drive on Moscow, but I know the group that went south eventually ended up tragically at Stalingrad.

Our problems with weather began before winter arrived, which starts very early in Russia. When the first snow fell in October, I could only think of the fate of Napoleon.* We had problems with the early snow, and as it started to melt, the so-called roads were nothing less than a swamp. And it rained and continued to rain. These were conditions we had not encountered in Poland or France. I was assigned again to drive the motorcycle and sidecar, and had to go about sixty kilometers with a message. It took me a week to make the round trip. I was nearly pushing the motorcycle the whole way. Unimaginable.†

It was before winter arrived, not spring, the in-between period. Food transport trucks got stuck in the swampy roads, and emphasis appeared to be on delivery of ammunition and fuel so we could fight. On military maps we compared the Russian roads to our *Autobahn*, or superhighways, and

---

* The specter and failure of Napoleon was not lost on me and my comrades. As history well records, exactly 129 years before Hitler launched the attack on the Soviet Union, Bonaparte invaded Russia, but after entering Moscow was beaten back into France by the Czar's armies and the Russian winter.

† A most appropriate description of the October rains follows. (I remember it well.) It turned tracks into "oozing quagmires and the fields into seas of jelly three feet or more deep. The mud sucked up guns and baggage, drew boots off the soldiers and halted vehicles. Trucks and wagons sank to their axles in it, horses to their bellies....For want of fuel the tanks stalled; for want of ammunition the guns fell silent; for want of food the troops went hungry." [Nicholas Bethell and the Editors of Time-Life Books, *Russia Besieged* (Alexandria, Va.: Time-Life Books, 1977), 164]

Soviet fighter destroyed by German fire. 1941.

The horizon goes on forever in this flat Russian landscape, but this Soviet bi-plane fighter will not. 1941.

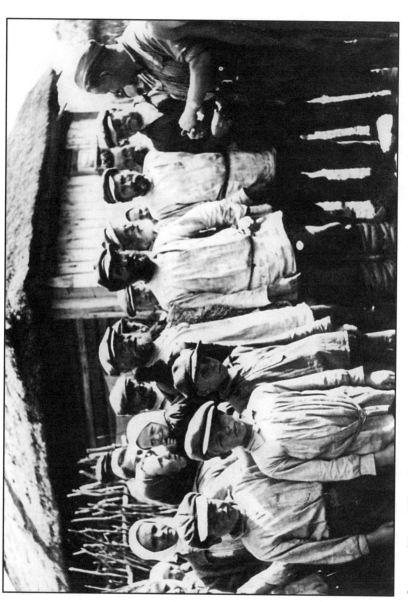

A committee of Russian peasants gathers to welcome Frisch's unit to their village. 1941.

A crowd of curious Germans gathers at the wreckage of a Russian T-34/76 42 tank. 1941.

The company street in Frisch's battery's tent encampment. Soviet Union, Summer 1941.

Frisch's battery rests along with its 10cm gun cradled in limber. Soviet Union, 1941.

Strassen, or streets. In Russia an *Autobahn* was when we were up to our ankles in dirt or mud. On *Strassen* we were up to our knees. In short, Russian roads, if they could be called that, were the perfect troop stopper to all organized movement.[*]

The smells of danger were everywhere—enemy guns, aircraft, artillery shells, and a sound only known in Russia which was "Stalin's pipe organ."[†] The Russians had a set of eight rockets shooting at the same time from this Stalin organ launcher. This was the most shocking and terrifying thing I ever encountered. The only good thing about the Stalin organ was the beautiful smoke fan appearing at the rear, which gave away its position. We could do something to retaliate if we only had enough ammunition. The sounds were terrible, terrible. We encountered the Katyusha the first time after Smolensk. For a long time it seemed the rockets would never end.

Another danger was coming. I will never forget this. We were on the Smolensk defense line. We were told we were going to capture Moscow by December 1941. There was a German intelligence officer, General Gehlen,[‡]

---

[*] October 2 was Hitler's "unrealistic" target date for starting the all-out assault on Moscow, Operation *Taifun* (Typhoon). Nearly thirty divisions were transferred to Army Group Center, clogging the already congested muddy roads leading east, and causing tremendous logistical and command problems.

[†] The Katyusha rocket launcher, an early Soviet secret weapon, was effective and devastating to German troop morale.

[‡] General Reinhard Gehlen, chief of intelligence on the Eastern Front.

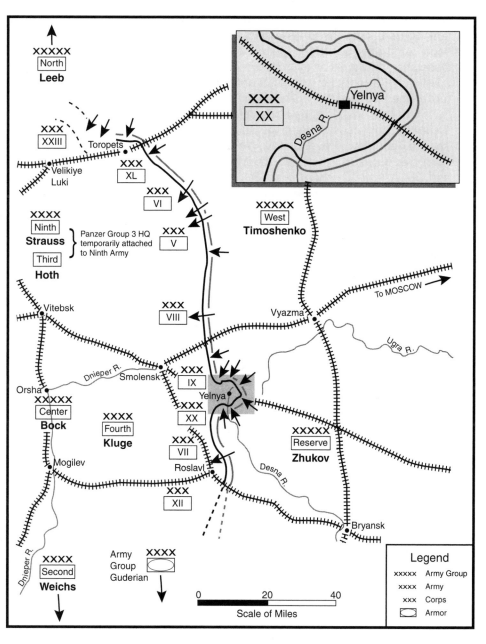

Yelnya salient lines near Smolensk, Russia, August–September 1941.

Standing Fast: German Defensive Doctrine on the Russian Front During World War II
(U.S. Army Command and General Staff College)

who reportedly predicted the Russians were mobilizing a completely new tank corps behind the Urals, using the new T-34 tank. The T-34 would soon come after us, and it spearheaded the Russian counteroffensive in December, driving us away from Moscow. Our men were terrified of the T-34. It was superior to our tanks or anti-tank weapons. We knew we had to move when we saw the T-34s. It was a clear message.

Our drive in the center front on Moscow began in early October. With some luck, our forces defeated the Russians in the area of Bryansk-Vyazma, and we kept moving ever slowly. We advanced along the direction of the highways between Smolensk and Moscow through the areas of Kaluga and Obninskoye. To my recollection we were assigned most of the time to Hoeppner's Fourth *Panzergruppe*. By late November our advance had bogged down due to a combination of weather, temperature, supply, fatigue, and the Red Army, who were unwilling to let us get any closer. We saw the streetcars in the outskirts of Moscow, but we did not fire any rounds into Moscow. It was too far away.* We of course did not then realize it, but our army had stopped its assault. What we did know was that we had to ready our positions and begin to prepare for the freezing cold. From then on we would have to fight to hold what we had, or we would have to fight to prevent the enemy from running over us as we backed up toward the west.

At that time, the German army, famous for *Panzers* and motorized forces, was operating very erratically due to many mechanical problems. Some motorized units were no longer mobile, thanks—not to the Russians—but to the weather. We also had to depend on horse-drawn vehicles to bring supplies from the railroads distant to the rear. Because of the extremely cold temperatures, often below minus 30 degrees Celsius, or about 22 degrees below zero Fahrenheit, many trucks, some of our guns, and other vehicles developed "cold breaks" in the leaf springs. They just wouldn't run. Thirty percent of the leaf springs in our trucks broke. If one broke in the rear, the truck lost braking capacity. It wouldn't stop. The German army started in a hurry to put together truck repair shops for springs, but we didn't have enough materials or the right quality steel to make reliable springs. It meant we started the offensive on Moscow with dilapidated equipment, and we lost a lot of it. Remember, our guns in the *Panzers* were all pulled by vehicles. The horse-drawn artillery belonged to plain infantry divisions.

There was something else. During this cold no truck would start. But if a unit was able to capture somewhere on the way a Russian truck, those

---

* Bryansk-Vyazma in early October was one of the largest German victories in the campaign and yielded some 550,000 prisoners in the defeat of six Soviet armies. German pincers forced the enemy into creating a new defense line to protect Moscow. For about five weeks in October-November, rains stalled the assault, giving the Soviets time to build defenses and augment the troops. By the end of November, when the ground hardened under freezing temperatures, Bock's advance parties got to within thirty-two kilometers (twenty miles) of the Soviet capital. Optimism was premature, for we had reached the limits of our endurance.

bastards were so simple you could fix the carburetor and make a fire under the engine. Then we cranked the truck, and as soon as the Russian truck was running, we started to pull the German truck. The Russian trucks were of an ancient design. There was not a screw on the Russian trucks you could take off without the vehicle falling apart. It was the most primitive design—approximately a Ford Model A—that can be imagined, but the bastard was running always. We tried to capture Russian trucks as much as we could. It saved our lives.

No soldier could understand the idea of an offensive under such miserable conditions. The spirit of the troops was also below zero. We suffered terribly, as you know from reading the historical account. The wind blew almost all the time. We never officially received winter clothes and could not understand why they were not given to us. Our men received pieces from home in the mail, mostly socks. We improvised by wearing newspapers inside shoes and all our shirts and underwear at the same time, and tried making straw and rope boots to cover the shoes. Our clothes became infested with lice which added to the cold misery. Our skin was greasy and itchy. We dared not sweat too much, if that was possible, because it gave us a nasty chill in the wind.*

In our battery, only two out of four guns and about half of the ammunition trucks were moveable. Of course, I being a hopeful engineer learned my first lesson about the difference between performance and reliability: "The performance is fantastic, provided the mousetrap works." This was such interesting confusion that even officers were starting to ask the question, "What stupidity is this?"—to start an attack with units with trucks that wouldn't move, ammunition trucks with cold brakes and no springs. The units were not combat ready because of the lack of transportation. The faithful and industrious horses fared poorly in the cold, and could not pull half-tracks. The glorious leader Hitler got this idea for the last attack of the year, to take Moscow. He was absolutely crazy. But of course nobody dared to say this, and everybody was saying, "Yes, sir. *Heil* Hitler."†

---

* In the attached Sidebar I have included further details of the conditions we suffered on the Russian front and particularly during the winter of 1941. The Sidebar summarizes conditions described in the most accurate publications I have read on the subject, that tell it much better than I could attempt to do. The publications are postwar U.S. Army reports, written by German generals who were there, adjusted in the book *Fighting in Hell: The German Ordeal on the Eastern Front* (London and Mechanicsburg, Penn.: Greenhill Books and Stackpole Books, 1995), edited by Peter Tsouras. (The irony of the title of this book is that hell is hot, Russia was not.) The pamphlets of concern to me for this memoir are *Russian Combat Methods in World War II* (No. 20-2390) (Washington: Department of the Army, 1950); and *Effects of Climate on Combat in European Russia* (No. 20-291, 1952).

† One wonders what would have happened if we Germans had not pressed the assault on Moscow at the time and had waited out the winter somewhere else. Undoubtedly we would have had more supplies, and perhaps our winter clothing would have been delivered. But what about the Russians? In checking my statement, I read where Guderian and (General Franz) Halder (Chief of the Army General Staff *[OKH]*) tried to get Hitler to change his mind.

"General Winter": Our Enemy No. 2 in 1941[*]

The German soldier who crossed into Russian territory felt that he entered a different world, where he was opposed not only by the forces of the enemy but also by the forces of nature. Nature is the ally of the Russian Army....The winter of 1941-42 was most severe in European Russia [in a hundred years]. In the area northwest of Moscow the mean temperature during January 1942 was -32 degrees....The Russian peasant stores his winter supplies in advance and digs in to spend the winter completely cut off from the outside world....

Paralyzed by cold, the German troops could not aim their rifle fire, and bolt mechanisms jammed or strikers shattered....Machine guns became encrusted with ice, recoil liquid froze in guns, ammunition supply failed....Leadership and bravery could not compensate for the lowered firepower....Hitler neither expected nor planned for a winter war.

Night temperatures dropped to between -30 and -40 degrees, and no shelter was available to the German troops [on the Lama]....Periods of moderate cold alternating with thaw are particularly dangerous....Boots, socks, and trousers that had become wet during the day stiffened with the night cold and froze toes and feet. Serious frost injuries developed when troops overheated from combat were forced to spend the night in snow pits or windswept open fields, especially when the fatigued men took even the shortest of naps....

Frostbite was frequent among drivers and troops who were moved long distance in open trucks. So long as a suitable clothing was not available, constant indoctrination in cold-weather precautions was necessary. Frequent halts were made so men could warm themselves by exercise. Front-line troops became indifferent in extreme cold; under constant enemy pressure they became mentally numbed....Some chemical heat packets were issued but they protected only small areas of the body for short periods. Regular use of the sauna...was helpful in preventing illnesses...but such baths were not always available....

Artillery was moved on existing roads, and if no roads were available, new tracks were shoveled....The effectiveness

---

[*] This information is from *Effects of Climate on Combat in European Russia*, *op. cit.*, 146-65, 212. The report was prepared by a committee of former German generals and general staff officers under supervision of the U.S. Army (European Command) historical office. The principal author is *Generaloberst* Erhard Rauss, Commander, 3rd and 4th *Panzer* Armies.

of artillery projectiles, particularly those of small caliber, and mortar ammunition, was seriously hampered by deep snow [which] dampened and reduced lateral fragmentation of artillery shells....Heavy artillery weapons...remained highly effective....Registration fire with aerial observation and with flash and sound was hampered because the snow swallowed projectiles and bursts. Artillery map firing was impeded by a vast difference between meteorological conditions in Russia and in Central Europe. Metro corrections of German observation battalions were computed according to Central European standards, resulting in less accurate fire....By placing fire control and radio equipment in improvised wooden containers padded with blankets it was possible to protect them against frost damage and shock....

The Russian winter covers roads, countryside, and vehicles with a crippling coat of ice and, when sand is not available, entire columns are forced to halt. Icy roads can rob an offensive of surprise or be fatal to a withdrawal....Fearful that the pursuing Russians [December retreat] would overtake and destroy the rear guard if time were spent in extricating each vehicle, the Germans loaded as much materiel as possible on trucks still serviceable, and put the remaining equipment to the torch....The retreat became a race from village to village....Attempts to obtain dirt from the blasted [temporary hole] shelters for sanding roads were useless because the explosions loosed great chunks of solidly frozen earth which could not be pulverized....

During the inactivity of the autumn 1941 muddy period fur pieces and felt boots were manufactured locally, purchased from civilians, or removed from dead Russian soldiers; but these sources supplied only a small number of troops. All available underwear was issued so that several sets could be worn one at a time, and each man managed to obtain a piece of cloth for use as a belly-band or head protector....

The need for spare motor vehicle and tank parts increases at low temperatures. The number of broken springs...reached unusually high proportions. The Germans cannibalized broken-down and abandoned vehicles to get spare parts....Winter temperatures...render self-starters useless. The Germans resorted to prewarming engineers by building fires under them. In this way a few vehicles were started for towing....Most of the German horses became accustomed...although they needed at least emergency shelter. In the open, horses freeze to death at temperatures under -4 degrees....Germans expected their draft horses to pull excessive loads in winter, and the animals became prematurely spent particularly when they were given insufficient care, forage, and water....[Horses] frequently lacked winter shoeing...which caused them to fall....

The reverses suffered at Moscow lowered the morale of both officers and men who felt that lack of preparation for winter warfare was the cause of their defeat....Many men who had become separated from their units marched westward singly or in small groups and, when apprehended, freely admitted that their destination was Germany because "the war is over." These men were turned over to the nearest combat unit for rehabilitation....Since gasoline was precious, thefts of fuel were common [including from unattended tanks]....Spare parts were scarce and were stolen whenever it was opportune to do so.

[Conclusions] In 1941 the *Wehrmacht* did not recognize this force [climate] and was not prepared to withstand its effects. Crisis upon crisis and unnecessary suffering were the result. Only the ability of the German soldiers to bear up under misfortune prevented disaster. But the German Army never recovered from its first hard blow.

Contrasts in weather in Byelorussia. Taking time out for some water sports in the summer, during the successful early campaign. Soviet Union, 1941.

Russian citizens knew how to dress for the winter. We wished we could have bartered for their clothes, but it was forbidden—and besides, they smelled horrible. 1941.

German artillery trucks with broken springs or frozen engines sit waiting for either replacement springs, a fire beneath them, or a primitive captured Soviet truck to pull them for a start. Winter 1941.

Something far less than the French chateaus: the German army occupied peasant farmhouses as shelter from the Russian winter. Pictures on walls were never of friends, but of movie stars perhaps. "Nobody would have put family pictures on a wall like that," Frisch remembered. 1941.

Lacking adequate winter boots, German soldiers make snowshoes out of rope coverings to ward off the freezing weather. Russia, 1941.

On occasion visibility was reduced to practically zero from the miserable blowing snow. If we were a little bit in the rear we would be stationed in a village, really a collection of a few peasant farmhouses. It was our best means of surviving the cold, because we could not dig or construct outside shelters in the frozen ground except crudely by dynamiting holes. Each farmhouse consisted of two rooms. One room had a big stove, and there were bunks for sleeping above it. The other room was for a goat, a cow, a pig, and the outhouse. We had to dig things out and make our own place out of it inside the Russian farmhouse. If I had the watch I couldn't stand outside for longer than twenty minutes. After twenty minutes the next guy came out to relieve and then he was freezing. I'm not sure exactly what we were supposed to be watching out for; not even a Russian soldier would be around on those nights. It was simply unimaginable. But the interesting thing was all the farmhouses still had a religious icon, mostly behind a curtain. Some German soldiers removed the icons if the house was unoccupied. Occasionally we took one, but most of them were left there. If a Russian was in the house no German would touch the icons.

We had no idea how poor Russian farmers could be until we started living their lifestyle. Their farmhouses were only basic shelter. I have never again in my life seen primitive buildings as in Smolensk—just unbelievable. We had the feeling we were in a different world. My impression of Russia was that it was absolutely hopeless, enclosed in its own domain and should

In the simple peasant farmhouse quarters, a German soldier uses time to catch up on newspapers from home. Note the kerosene-type lamp hanging from ceiling. Russia, 1941.

stay there. Often I wondered just what was I, what were we, doing there? Why did we need Russia? What possible good could it do for us?

It was bad enough during the previous summer when we had to sleep outdoors. Then as winter was compelling us to seek shelter inside we saw the poverty even more so firsthand. The Russian peasant had no equivalent in the Western world, except perhaps in a poor farmer's barnyard. So we covered ourselves up with anything we had just to stay somewhat warm in their houses. We used bed covers, tablecloths, curtains, anything at all to provide a layer of warmth. It was not beyond us to remove boots and clothing from dead soldiers of both sides. When I was inside there was little to do except read and improve my chess playing and try not to think about being cold, until it was my turn to stand guard outside.

I do not believe Stalin's "scorched earth policy" was followed too closely by those officials who were ordered to carry it out, unless someone wanted to keep warm for a while. People, even subjects of the Soviet collectivist state, wanted to survive, and self-destruction was of little survival value. If we burn it, guess what? The Germans can't have it now, and we can't have it later. There comes a point where even fanatics start to use their brain.

I saw lots of Russian peasants, and they did not treat us unkindly. They were dirty, certainly not attractive, and looked like pictures I had seen of ignorant poor farmers of the Czar's days with shirt-jackets tied at the waist, and large furry caps. I remember peasant fugitives coming through our lines, presumably from the front. They were human beings, in spite of their appearance. We offered them the so-called warmth of our house—which we had "borrowed" from some other farmers—for a while. Only a few times did they steal or try to steal something from us, but never our weapons. But their personal habits reached back to life even far before the first czar. We could not believe it. They used their own trousers as toilets, and after five minutes in the room we had to run out because we couldn't take the smell anymore, in spite of the cold. I cannot describe it. We

A friendly descendant of Czar Peter the Great, or Ivan the Terrible, but somewhat worse for wear. Russia, winter 1941.

tried to sleep on straw or filthy wooden beds or whatever was there, and turn out any thoughts of comfort. We settled for just being happy to wake up every morning and still be alive.

For subsistence sometimes we went into the woods and tried to dig out mushrooms if we could find any. Every soldier had a sack with him for potatoes and onions. We tried to dig them out wherever we could and then roasted them. We had no butter; so we sometimes put them in a pan with some water over the fire. At least they got warm. Starting fires and keeping them going also required persistent searches for something to burn. For a certain time the supply system collapsed completely and we were on our own. Whatever little there was to be taken, we took. Animals did not live long. If an animal or bird was around we immediately grabbed it for food. Blizzards with deep blowing and drifting snow covered so much it was impossible to find items to forage, including wood. We could not obtain fresh water from wells; the contents were frozen and polluted. So we had to resort to melting snow, one luxury which was at least an inexhaustible supply.

During the early December retreat from the Moscow suburbs, or "front readjustment," I got frostbite in my right leg while riding my motorcycle carrying messages.* I froze my leg a little bit, not too much, but just enough to be recognized. There was no way to prevent it. I had been wearing all the clothes I possibly could. I had not been driving the motorcycle at a fast speed because of the roads; so I believe what caused the frostbite was contact with the frozen machine and being exposed too long. It happened about three weeks before Christmas. Fortunately I was retired from the front toward a rear medical station for treatment. I was lucky in that my case was severe enough to get me off the front awhile, but I must say my leg has bothered me ever since.†

Artillery Regiment 109 was relieved by another unit and withdrawn right before Christmas 1941 and sent home. We had to leave almost all our guns, vehicles, and equipment in place because we had little means of delivering it when we left. We were sent home on trains, and although we got no new clothing and meager rations on the trip, at least the cars were warmer than peasants' houses. And they smelled better, and we were able to sleep some sitting up on halfway comfortable seats.

---

* The Soviets launched their huge counterattack on December 5–6 under Marshal Georgi Zhukov, who would stay on the German heels into the heart of Berlin three and one-half years later. The German forces, weak and overextended, were easily routed. By the time Artillery Regiment 109 had left the front, our forces were about fifty miles farther away from Moscow.

† "General Winter" had begun to take control of the front. Our men of course were not used to such extremes. To be wounded or injured in the snow invited death from shock and exposure. Men checked each other for frostbite and looked especially at feet, hands, and head. Symptoms were treated crudely with heat, but often men had to stay on duty. Some men lost limbs, and I heard that something like nearly 113,000 cases occurred before December was over. Severe cases appeared to resemble gangrene. During the entire winter nearly 100,000 German horses were lost to the cold, but their flesh became a delicacy for attentive soldiers.

Soldier ventures down into shell crater while observers cast shadows from the rim. Russia, 1941.

At this time I got my first furlough period home to study one semester at the Technical University in Vienna. Here again I was very lucky. It was a nice break while recovering from the frostbite, and a joyous reward for having spent upwards of two-plus years away on campaign or preparing for campaign. It was my first time at the university from where I would ultimately receive my degree. It was an enjoyable and beautiful experience. Yet my thoughts were with our comrades who by now were being pushed back steadily from Moscow, never to see it again.

After the December retreat, where my regiment had lost everything, once we were removed from the Eastern Front we went back to Czechoslovakia to regroup, train, and be reconstituted with new replacement men and equipment. I rejoined them in the late spring of 1942, once my semester was completed.

Watching the Eastern Front developments as we were, and trying to ascertain the real truth from what little half-truths (or lies) we were told, my friends and I reached certain conclusions. Although we soldiers were not giving up, the war had taken a turn against Germany by then, and we speculated privately—very privately—about the future. Looking back now, from my viewpoint, I strongly suspect, but cannot prove, that the calamity in winter 1941—not 1942—in front of Moscow decided the war for us. The German industry was unable to replace the winter losses prior to the offensives in 1942 with the result that the calamity of 1941 ultimately brought on the catastrophic surrender in January 1943 at Stalingrad. The losses of soldiers, machines, and equipment at Moscow were irreplaceable. I have never seen anything written about this point. More than two decades later and in retrospect, this led to my extreme thesis that an army cannot lose more in a day than the industry can produce or replace in a day. I brought up my thesis a few years ago before the end of the Cold War in a global war game where industry experts with computer models assured us that all losses can easily be compensated for within two or three years. Two or three years? What enemy will wait that long? Certainly not the Red Army.

There are certain moments of my sixth-month experience in the Soviet Union from June 22 to late December 1941 that I can never forget or describe well. Perhaps the most dramatic one happened earlier in Russia when the assault unit we were supporting put together a reconnaissance-in-force, with one artillery battery of four 10cm guns, and a motorcycle battalion of infantry. This reconnaissance-in-force was to proceed ahead of our position to learn the enemy strength, and come back and report to

Frisch's battery *Kapitaen*. **Russia, 1941.**

headquarters. Our group, with me as a member, went through our own infantry lines with the order to go as far as we could before encountering resistance. From the moment we went through the lines, we knew we were completely alone. No one spoke. I remember the men in the infantry looked at us in the battery like we were crazy. Suddenly I felt I was alive, I wanted to be alive, but at the same time I had the feeling we were going into a death trap. It is awfully hard to describe the feeling I had in moments like that, this moment when we entered enemy territory in total silence. We found out what we needed to, and we returned.

The other instance which brought forth feelings I cannot describe was in 1939 in Poland when we heard about the British-French ultimatum over German involvement in Poland. Those were the two moments when no one spoke. Everybody had his own ideas and I don't know what everybody thought. It also had the quietness of a death trap. I will never forget these absolutely haunting pictures.

When the retreat from Moscow began, I felt it was the end. Yet, the motto of our service in Russia was: "You have to have a positive attitude." Still, everybody in my regiment who left with me was happy and morale was pretty high. Most of us had made it out alive and would fight again somewhere else.

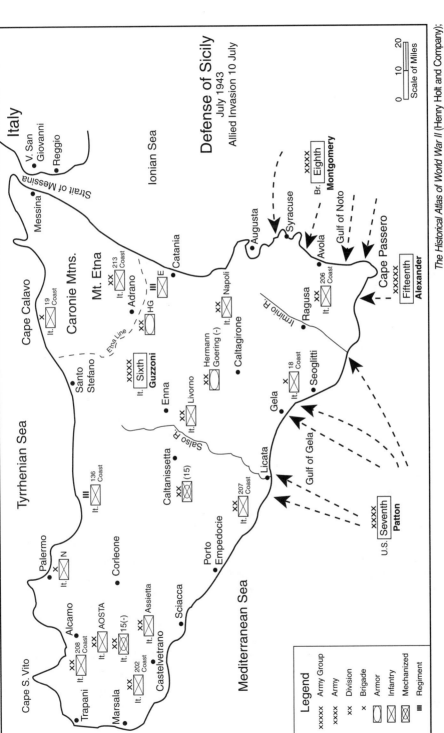

Defense of Sicily
July 1943
Allied Invasion 10 July

Italy

V. San Giovanni
Reggio

Strait of Messina

Messina

Cape Calavo

Caronie Mtns.

Mt. Etna

Santo Stefano

Enna Line

Tyrrhenian Sea

Cape S. Vito

Palermo

It. | N

Alcamo

Corleone

It. | 208 Coast
It. | AOSTA
It. | 15(-)
It. | Assietta

Castelvetrano

It. | 202 Coast

Trapani

Marsala

Sciacca

Porto Empedocie

It. | 207 Coast

Caltanissetta

It. | (15)

It. | 136 Coast

Salso R.

Enna

It. | Livorno

Mediterranean Sea

Licata

Gulf of Gela

Gela

It. | 18 Coast

Seoglitti

Ragusa

Simto R.

Seoglitti

Caltagirone

It. | Napoli

It. | Hermann Goering (-)

HG

III | E

It. | 213 Coast

Adrano

Catania

Augusta

Syracuse

Ionian Sea

Gulf of Noto

Avola

Cape Passero

It. | 206 Coast

xxxxx | Fifteenth
Alexander

xxxx | Br. Eighth
Montgomery

xxxx | Sixth
Guzzoni

It. | 19 Coast

u.s. | xxxx Seventh
Patton

Legend

xxxxx   Army Group
xxxx   Army
xx   Division
x   Brigade
    Armor
    Infantry
    Mechanized
III   Regiment

The Historical Atlas of World War II (Henry Holt and Company);
Atlas for the Second World War (The West Point Military History Series);
Atlas of the Second World War (Geographia); *The Italian Campaign* (Time-Life Books)

Scale of Miles
0   10   20

Chapter 4

Feldzug in Sizilien und Italien, 1942–45,
und Kriegsgefangenschaft, 1945–47
Campaigns in Sicily and Italy, 1942–45,
and Prisoner of War, 1945–47

One thing which is hard for me to understand, and for everybody, was the cautiousness of the American troops. When we retreated from the valley which goes to Monte Cassino we couldn't understand why we were not followed by American troops. We turned around and nobody was behind us anymore. There were no weather problems. We didn't stop to find out why.

After leaving the Soviet Union, and completing our reconstitution and training in Czechoslovakia in 1942, our regiment was transferred to a camp in Osnabrueck, Germany. There we got a lot of new recruits for training—basic training without guns. In this place, we all had to undergo a medical examination. We were thinking it was routine, but it was much more: It was an examination for fitness for duty in a "tropical climate."

Shortly thereafter our unit was split up. Those men fit for the so-called tropical service, including me, got transferred to the newly reconstituted Artillery Battalion *(Artillerie Abteilung)* 557. Those not fit for tropical service, including a number of my friends and comrades over the years, were placed back in the former *Artillerie Abteilung* 109. Redesignated Artillery Regiment *Gross Deutschland*, this old unit 109 was eventually completely destroyed in the Battle of Stalingrad. My new unit, 557, already began to wear the North African desert uniform of Rommel's *Afrika Korps.*

First we went by ship to Naples, Italy, in summer 1942, where we entered an acclimatization camp to get used to the Mediterranean weather. It is needless for me to say that this climate change was welcomed after being in Russia. Those who had been through that nightmare certainly believed we had earned it. The acclimatization camp was constructed

100

Frisch, sighting transit, during training in land measurement for artillery spotting. Germany, 1942.

around a sports arena near the old Roman town of Pozzuoli. The camp also turned out to be my first prisoner of war (POW) camp after the war. Little did I imagine I would return there under such conditions. We worked hard in Naples in preparation for whatever was scheduled next, but we thoroughly enjoyed Naples, its beauty, its women, the Marsala wine, and the espresso, and our camp around the sports arena. The relaxed and less stressful situation reminded me somewhat of my earlier days two years before in Rheims.

The time in the acclimatization camp was tremendously enjoyable. I became the leader of an artillery calculating group called the *Rechentrupp*. An explanation: These are the people who measure for the location of the guns—like a land surveyor—and calculate the elevations, influence of weather, wind, and temperature, and give the necessary correction for gun adjustment. It was my first and only assignment with leadership authority. Had they forgiven my wicked past? I think the answer was I was one of the few experienced veterans around.

I had two new recruit privates in my group. One was a lawyer from Styria, in Austria, Dr. August (nickname "Gustel") Pendel, and the other was curator of the National Museum of Art in Vienna, Dr. Lothar Kitchelt. Within no time, the two doctors and I became the best of friends. Both were much older than I. Unfortunately, Lothar got killed in the Italian campaign, and Gustel died of old age about ten years after the war.

The three of us explored Naples, Capri, Pompei, and Salerno. Gustel was an expert in wines, espresso, and music. Lothar explored with us all available places of art, from churches to excavations. And I entertained them with stories of Italian racing cars and motorcycles. We had complete trust in each other. We talked about our families and shared political heresy. We enjoyed Italy, its wine, the climate, and learned Italian as much as we could, while most of our German comrades complained bitterly about the lack of cleanliness, the lack of discipline in traffic, and other Southern Italian customs. Hah! Just adjust, my friends, was what I would tell them. Keep your hands on your money, keep your eyes open for the honking automobiles and the horse carts, and smell the lovely sunshine. And see, no snow.

The fun in Italy, at least around Naples, ended for me approximately October 1942, when I was stricken heavily with jaundice, together with

Naples, Italy, 1942. Two new privates of 1st Battery who became Frisch's friends: Dr. August "Gustel" Pendel *(left)*, a Styria, Austria, lawyer, and Dr. Lothar Kitchelt, curator of the National Museum of Art in Vienna. The three explored Naples and surrounding area together, enjoying culture, food and wine. Kitchelt was killed during the Italian campaign in 1943.

about a dozen others, from eating Neapolitan shellfish. My precautions had failed me for once. We were packed into a Lazarett train and sent to a hospital in Bavaria. There I fell into the hands of a bright young medical doctor. I assumed he was a medical efficiency expert. He told me: "We should use your time for recuperation from the jaundice to take care of your varicose veins." What could I say? So I got my injections—but the young doctor missed the veins—and the injection went into the muscle, and bruised me so badly that I could not walk. I could have complained about the doctor's incompetence which would have harmed his career. But I kept my mouth shut and got four months *Heimaturlaub*, which was vacation at home to recuperate after the hospital. The doctor, so I assume, invented a reason not detrimental to his career, and I then was able to take a second semester at the Technical University in Vienna. Frostbite and jaundice in four years in the army, but no bullet holes. It occurred to me as I ended the year 1942, that it had been the first whole year since 1938, when I entered the military, I had not fought in battle.

It was a beautiful time due to private reasons. It was an exciting time because of the opportunity to learn, but it was also a shocking time, because of the news from the front in Stalingrad. The majority of the old *Artillerie Regiment* 109 were there. Among them, my best friend since the first day in the military, Franzi Mahr. He was an only child and engaged to a girl in a small village in the Rhineland near Koeln. Our unit (109) was there in quarters before the campaign in France.

When the German army in Stalingrad surrendered in February 1943, about ninety-five thousand German soldiers went into captivity. Years later, long after the war's end, approximately five thousand returned home. My friend Franzi was not among them, and shortly thereafter his parents died of a broken heart, as we might say. About my friend's bride-to-be: Almost fifty years later, I visited her. She was married to an invalid of the war. We did not talk about my friend. We looked in each other's eyes and understood each other...eyes which could not shed tears anymore. I had more Franzis during the war who did not make it, but none so dear to me as he.

Approximately at the end of March 1943, I returned to my unit, the 1st Battery of Artillery Battalion 557. It was located near the airport in Palermo, Sicily, and I reached there by rail, boat, and truck. The 1st Battery was all what was left from the Battalion 557. The 2nd Battery had been detached for the *Afrika Korps* and made it down to Tunis, North Africa, but after the landing had the misfortune to lose a battle, and went in best organized form into an American POW camp. And the 3rd Battery faired much worse, and still rests somewhere on the bottom of the Mediterranean after being torpedoed on the transport from Sicily to Tunis. Only the 1st Battery survived—and was again the core for a new 557, employed first in Sicily, and then in Italy to the bitter end.

I might consider myself very lucky to have missed assignment to the 2nd or 3rd Batteries, but instead I felt strongly from this time on my place in the German army was simply: Condemned to die—condemned to live.

From there we went down to prepare for what we believed would be an inevitable Allied forces landing, and were now stationed in the area of Castelvetrano in southwestern Sicily, about six miles inland from the Mediterranean coast. There the Americans made the biggest mistake in their life. We prepared all our artillery positions in the direction of Trapani-Marsala area on the western coast, where the German army expected the American landing. But the Americans were careless enough to land in the south in the Gulf of Gela, however, and the British in the eastern area in Catania and Syracuse, practically behind our front where we had laid out our artillery positions, but miles away.[*]

When they landed behind us—the date was July 10, 1943—we began running like crazy for Messina to get across the straits into Italy. The Italian army shattered like glass and left much of the fighting to defend their territory to us Germans. (Besides, had we been able to stay in Sicily, the wine in Marsala would have been much better than the wine in Salerno, which is the area where we were headed and where we would be when the Allies made their landings there on the boot of Italy. In fact, the Americans for all intents bypassed Marsala.) Unfortunately, therefore, we never did make it to North Africa. So much for tropical acclimatization. But the story of the German forces was not too good there either. Take your pick. Either way we moved backward.

One thing to remember was that the fighting positions and tactics of the German army in Europe had changed radically. We were no longer operating as armored attacking forces, as when we were overrunning France. Now we had become defenders. In Sicily and Italy we fought a defensive war that meant frequently adjusting our lines, virtually always going backward. This was also our first time fighting the Americans. We wondered what they were like, and how we would react.

As soon as we got our guns positioned, it seemed the advancing Allies forced us to withdraw quickly. Both the German and Italian armies were being forced by Allied advances northeastward toward the only obvious place to go, Messina. A bottleneck was forming to some extent. The Italian army got in our way, some wished to surrender to the Americans; the Sicilians got in our way, and after a few days of fighting we knew the smartest thing for us to do was to evacuate the island. I believe our route

---

[*] We Germans numbered about 60,000 of the 240,000 Axis troops on Sicily. The force was commanded by General (Alfredo) Guzzoni of the Italian Sixth Army. We were there to prop them up, but before the landings they already looked ragged and demoralized, and lacked proper fighting equipment. Our first news of the Allies was that paratroopers had landed the night of July 9. My battery remained in Castelvetrano long enough to fire a few rounds at Americans advancing up the coast from Licata; then we pulled back northeastward ahead of them.

Kapitaen Mack, *center*, in the sunshine, musters 1st Battery, Artillery Battalion 557, in Sicily, 1943.

Frisch comrade and mascot monkey relax in Sicily, 1943.

followed across the Mazzara Mountains toward Bagheria and Termini, then along the Tyrrhenian coast.*

Our unit incurred only a few casualties, and I doubt we caused many ourselves. Some days we made better time and distance than others, but we never did remain in any place long enough to put up a pitched defense. Token resistance is a term I learned which identified closely with our efforts. I think the mountains and terrible roads hindered the Americans as much or more than our guns. I believe our commanders, and certainly soldiers at our level, figured there was not much sense in trying to hold on to Sicily: Let's get over to Italy where we can regroup and build better defenses and stay longer.†

We had to retreat very rapidly as much as we could toward Messina. Once there, we boarded boats, including landing craft, to ferry our men, guns, and equipment across the three-or-so miles of the Strait of Messina

---

* Much of the effort to slow down the Americans came from German engineers who destroyed or mined bridges, tunnels, and roads. The only tactical advantage we had was using the natural terrain of barren hills, valleys, and steep ridges. This brief experience would help us in later battles in Italy.

† From August 11–17, the German and Italian forces were evacuated across the Strait of Messina. U.S. Lieutenant General (George S.) Patton's Seventh Army, which we had faced, captured the final objective, Messina, on the seventeenth, just missing our rear guards. British General (Sir Bernard) Montgomery's Eighth Army came up from the south two hours later. Sicily, a wasted and fruitless military effort for our unit, fell that day. The Germans saved some 40,000 men, 50 tanks, 100 guns (including our battery), and many supplies to fight with again.

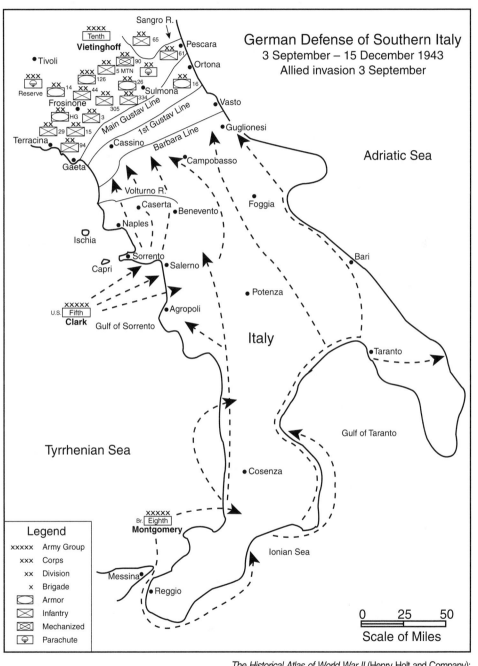

German Defense of Southern Italy
3 September – 15 December 1943
Allied invasion 3 September

Sangro R.

XXXX Tenth
Vietinghoff

XX 65

XX 61

Pescara

•Tivoli

XX 90
5 MTN

XX

Ortona

XXX
126

XX 26

XXX

•Sulmona

XX 16

XXX
Reserve

XX 14

XX 44
XX
334

XX 305

•Frosinone

XX HG

XX 3

Main Gustav Line

1st Gustav Line

•Vasto

XX 29

XX 15

Barbara Line

•Guglionesi

Terracina

XX 94

•Cassino

Adriatic Sea

Gaeta

•Campobasso

Volturno R.

•Caserta

•Benevento

•Foggia

•Naples

Ischia

Sorrento

•Bari

Capri

XXXXX
U.S. Fifth
Clark

•Salerno

•Potenza

•Agropoli

Gulf of Sorrento

Italy

•Taranto

Gulf of Taranto

Tyrrhenian Sea

•Cosenza

XXXXX
Br. Eighth
Montgomery

Ionian Sea

Legend

xxxxx	Army Group
xxx	Corps
xx	Division
x	Brigade
	Armor
	Infantry
	Mechanized
	Parachute

Messina•

•Reggio

0   25   50

Scale of Miles

The Historical Atlas of World War II (Henry Holt and Company);
Atlas for the Second World War (The West Point Military History Series);
Atlas of the Second World War (Geographia)

into Calabria in Southern Italy. We did not stop to fire at the Allies in Messina after we reached Italy, but reorganized and drove immediately north toward the Bay of Naples. We dodged many air attacks along the coast road.

We passed Salerno, not stopping, and continued on to Naples itself. Therefore, we were not involved in the defense of Salerno when the Allies invaded there on September 9.* We were stationed outside of Naples to the north near Caserta, near the Volturno River, and there our front line in Italy froze for the first time. We built our positions and waited. In late September, the Americans broke away from the Salerno area and approached Naples. As the city fell on October 1, we were doing some serious fighting trying to hold the line. The Volturno defense line gave the Germans some room to breathe, and we held for a few days.

From the Volturno we moved northward to form the Gustav Line in the Liri River Valley along the Garigliano and Rapido Rivers and the town of Cassino and its neighboring monastery, Monte Cassino. Cassino was approximately fifty miles north of Naples. It seemed like after Naples, my unit was setting up defense lines in intervals of approximately one hundred kilometers. The Gustav Line would prove to be one of Germany's most formidable defense lines of the war, and we held off the Allies in a bloody and treacherous continuing battle at Cassino for months, from mid-January to mid-May 1944. It was the largest and bloodiest battle of the Italian campaign. We spent a cold and horrid winter at Cassino with no relief. As bad as it was, let me tell you it was absolutely nothing like Russia. After Moscow, I could put up with most any deprivations. And I had to nonetheless. The Americans saw to it. We were no longer attached to a *Panzer* unit, and had not been for some time and would not again in the war because of the static and totally defensive nature of the Italian campaign. We were part of the German Tenth Army, the principal such German force in Italy. Our commander, General (Heinrich) von Vietinghoff, was a capable leader and would do his best devising our defense lines for the next twelve months.

For several weeks after mid-November there were few troop movements as we prepared for the enemy's attack. When the Allies landed behind our lines at Anzio on January 22, we were still in the Gustav Line. The Battle of Cassino was deadly, an awful, awful sight. The attrition reminded me of Smolensk and Bryansk-Vyazma; in one respect it was perhaps worse only because it lasted so much longer. There were times when our guns were in almost hourly use either repelling attacks or supporting our counterattacks, as long as we had ammunition.

---

* The British under Montgomery landed in Reggio Calabria in the "toe" and proceeded up the eastern side. The American Fifth Army, under (Lieutenant) General (Mark) Clark, came ashore in the Gulf of Salerno between Amalfi and Agropoli. For the next few months we faced the U.S. X and XI Corps in their drive up the western coast. Italy capitulated on September 3 and essentially pulled its armies from the field. Some units fought with the Allies.

Frisch, *second from left*, with German comrades, Poggio Berni, Italy, September 13, 1944. An inscription reads: "Because of my transfer from the staff [of Artillery Battalion 557] to the 3rd Battery, to my never tiring co-worker Frisch, in remembrance from his Lieutenant Haas." Haas is second from right.

In the early spring of 1944 when it became obvious the Monte Cassino area would fall, we moved out from Cassino in a southwesterly direction and couldn't go back, because the mountain ranges were directly north. So we were directed to move toward the coast to near Formia and Gaeta on the west coast, still behind the Gustav Line, and then were better able to go up the coast headed north. Our unit bypassed Rome and helped to form the next defense line north of Rome. After Cassino the front lines—we had always established two or three front lines behind where we had already selected the artillery positions—one after the other got chewed up, and we moved to the next, going north. Then we heard the news that Rome was taken on June 4, a great propaganda and political victory for the Allies. Hannibal was but the first great warrior to lust after Rome. The latest were Churchill and Eisenhower.

My unit moved from one defense line after the next without really noticing any particular pressure. I think what the German army tried to do was to pull out when preparation for an attack became evident. We fired on the enemy to harass them, but when necessary, fired on them with heavier intent to try to force them to change their plans. The British Eighth Army was coming up the eastern side of the boot, and the U.S. Fifth Army up the western side, separated in some places by the Apennine Mountains. I have seen the word "slog" used in respect to the pace and manner of the Allies in advancing in Italy. Slog applied also to the Germans, who with great effort slowed the enemy and kept him at bay during 1944. We were not without certain definite advantages: The country was made for defensive warfare, with continuous rocky hills and narrow passes and winding narrow roads, and we used the terrain everywhere. When we were through with a position, road, or bridge, on leaving we could disable it to hinder whoever tried to follow; and the winter cold, rains, and mud now welcomed the Allies like they had welcomed me to Russia in 1941.* The weather worked for and against both friend and foe, and in Italy it easily became the hated mutual foe of both sides.

We continued to establish semblances of defense lines, one across the boot between Pisa, Florence, and Arezzo to the Adriatic. When this was breached, we picked up our things and moved again, this time to form the so-called Gothic Line. It was a heavier-fortified line, in nothing but mountains, the Apennines, between near Carrara across the ridges to Pesaro near San Marino. The line held until mid-September. Once over the Gothic Line in September the Allies advanced quickly out of the hills toward the Po River Valley north of Bologna. From then on it seemed like the race was between their armored and motorized forces, and our feet. But by October, the rains, snow, and mud stopped them again, and the drive halted around the Gothic Line until spring.†

In April 1945, Vietinghoff went with *SS* General (Karl) Wolff to Switzerland to negotiate the surrender of our troops in Italy with American intelligence officer Allen Dulles. Vietinghoff and Wolff were both very much afraid of being shot if that became public—they still did not know what was going on in Germany—and they invented a marvelous method of capitulation. The way it worked was like this. Suddenly, the highest command post was on the move and couldn't be reached. The next highest command post of the corps was on the move and couldn't be reached. The command post of the divisions was on the move and couldn't be reached. This meant they dissolved the entire German army by eliminating the command posts,

---

* Again, the *Einfache Soldat* has to question where we are going and how we are going to get there. We kept looking for reenforcements to arrive from the north; some came, others kept being promised to Kesselring (Field Marshal Albert, commander of Army Group Southwest, i.e., Italy) and by Kesselring. As long as the supplies and ammunition were available to us in artillery, we could continue these delaying actions. But for what purpose? I doubt if our leaders ever thought for once we would turn around and head south and run them out of Italy. Hitler, of course, we understood would not tolerate large withdrawals northward to establish solid lines in the Northern Apennines or the Alps. Soon we started measuring how far, how long, until we ourselves were pushed out of Italy with no recourse—maybe back home into Austria—regardless of someone's hard and fast utterly senseless directives.

† By March of 1945, the Germans were down to twenty-six undermanned divisions to defend a long front as Italy got wider, relying on rivers and part of the old Gothic Line. The thoughtful Vietinghoff now primarily wanted to save as many men as possible from the inevitable complete breakthrough. After I was captured that month, the final line of consequence reached from Lake Garda to Ostiglia to the Adriatic. The official surrender of the German forces, a cease-fire, was agreed to on May 2. By then I was on my way to a POW camp in Pozzuoli near Naples.

The French Maginot Line, built between the world wars to keep the Germans out of France, but bypassed by modern armored warfare in 1940.

and the troops were saying, "What now? We can't reach anybody for instructions. Okay, let's walk home." Wolff, after the war, was the first commander of the police in Munich. I don't know if this was his price for taking such action.

My unit, or what was left of it, would never really find out that we had surrendered. We only knew that everybody was on his own and on the move. We were never aware of any organized surrender. This fact is not mentioned in historical accounts, and no one ever talks about it, a part of history about which very little is known. I can tell you only my theory. My interpretation is Vietinghoff and Wolff were afraid to talk about it to protect their lives because they knew what the *SS* and *Gestapo* were doing in Germany, including retribution against families. At the same time I believe the German General Staff also collapsed when they found out. It took them that long. At that moment it was just a complete command blunder, no communications at all. Essentially it was a case of the end of battalion commanders; the regimental commanders were gone, and the rest said, so okay, let's go home. This is my perception as I remember it. And I know nobody ever talked about it. I know from experience. I was in an artillery command post: all higher command posts just disappeared.

At this time most German soldiers looked for an opportunity to make it honorably into captivity. We slowly, yes, slowly felt the war looked very bad for Germany. The only thing which prolonged the war was the Morgenthau Plan, and when the Morgenthau Plan became known a lot of people were saying, we are dead anyhow, let's fight on. Remember that the U.S. secretary of treasury (Henry Morgenthau) proposed making an agricultural country out of Germany. I had the impression the Morgenthau Plan was the best propaganda tool for the *Nazis*, and had in my judgment, prolonged the war by several months. Also, there continued to be a strong concern over the insistence of the Allies on the unconditional surrender of Germany. This insistence reduced substantially the will of the German leaders (except in Italy Generals Vietinghoff and Wolff) to look for alternative ways to surrender with some conditions to protect troops, property, and rights. However, there were many people in Germany who would have been willing to agree to a fair peace agreement, I assume.

Before discussing my capture and POW experiences, I will add a note or two about living and fighting in Italy for nearly three years (add the two more years I spent as a POW there, and it becomes five). The war in Italy was absolutely a highly cultivated war. Everybody knew you don't shoot on Christmas Eve. When you had British troops you knew when tea time was on the other side, and you did not interrupt tea time with stupid shooting. We were more than happy to respect the tea time and Christmas, and not to irritate the other side. The respect from the Allies was mutual.

We usually had enough supplies except that artillery ammunition became a real problem in the winter of 1944–45. The Italian farmers helped us with food as we retreated. Actually, the Italians, and Sicilians, acted without exceptions as human beings. They did not care for Mussolini. We had practically no contact with the Italian army, and of course they disappeared after Italy's capitulation in 1943. It had been for Italy a relatively cold winter in 1945, and except for the harsh winters, the weather overall in Italy was excellent, and the roads were like France's: acceptable, and superb compared to Russia's. We slept mostly in farmhouses—primitive, but comfortable. The combat situation overall was bearable (if that is the right word when a soldier has no other choice), not as extreme as it had been in Russia.

My unit had already crossed the Po River in Northern Italy in mid to late April when I was captured somewhere in the area around Ostiglia. The spring offensive against the Gothic Line along the Apennines had begun during the first few days of April. At the time there was no organized defense, only scattered German units, fragments, and each tried to save its own ass—excuse me, if I express it so crudely, but that's the only way. My battery had been broken up, some had been lost, and others went in different directions in the confusion. I had pretty good maps and was hoping I could make it back to Austria.

At that time we had soldiers in the German army who were 14-, 15- and 16-year old boys. I called them "babies" and "boy scouts"; they were hardly grown up. But the Germans had to use them, and rounded them up and sent them to the front with a rifle and helmet. I saw only one or two actually fighting, but heard that some of them held their own. They, too,

Frisch with the son of the owner of the house where he was quartered prior to the campaign in France, at Hermesdorf bei Waldbroil near Koeln, Germany, January 28, 1940.

were frightened enough to scurry for the border, away from the Allies. On their way back home, a group of fifteen or so needed help and adopted me as their leader. I was with a couple of other privates from my unit at the time and agreed to have them join us. This was my second opportunity to lead during my army service, and I was not much better at it this time than before with the artillery unit. They must have seen in me someone who could guide them into the arms of their mothers. When they saw an old guy like me—I was the oldest—they must have seen a father image. I had my pistol and a little ammunition, but they had no weapons except some knives.

But these babies had not had proper training as soldiers and as we walked and ran fast soon began to complain. First they were too tired and couldn't walk, then they were too hungry, the whole thing was too hard, they needed a rest. I couldn't abandon those kids. I had gotten attached to them but wanted to move on. If I had told them "to heck with you" I could have made it alone into Austria, but not with all these boy scouts running behind me: "What shall we do now?, we need a rest, we can't walk." To make it worse, I heard there were Italian partisans in the area and we should stay clear of them. I did for a while, until it was almost too late, and my first encounter was not pleasant.

I also heard the Americans were capturing scattered German units in the areas I was crossing. It was every man for himself, no communications, only a few rumors from German soldiers moving as fast as I was toward home.* We made it almost to South Tirol and the foot of the Alps, I believe north of Ostiglia, which is about sixty or seventy miles north of Bologna. I had a few addresses of places where to hide in Austria, and figured I had to walk at least several days to reach the border. But what good would it have done me to get back to my native country? The Americans were fighting my country too, and they were sure to come across the border.

Having to take care of the boys cost me personally enough time so that finally we all were captured by Italian communist partisans, who blocked our further move north. This was approximately in late-April—the date escapes me, we just weren't keeping track. But I remember very well my only contact with Italian partisans. We were standing on the roads with our hands behind our neck, as they told us to do. I was scared and just knew they would kill us. The partisans could not agree among themselves who would have the honor of shooting us and argued for some time on what to do with their new captives. That time the distinct Italian personality trait we had come to know, their inability to reach a decision, worked to our advantage.

Soon an American tank came along. Marching in the front of this tank was an American sergeant, the first black man I ever saw, maybe 6

---

* In April 1945 the Italian partisans, many of them communists, were very active in Northern Italy. They liberated some areas, harassed our troops, spared installations from being destroyed. Nearly 150,000 Germans had given up since the spring offensive began. Those still not captured, like me, were heading for Tirol in Austria and Germany.

Artillery Regiment 109 conducts training session after fall of Poland. 1939.

Someone scored a direct hit on the dirt road, enough to detour the *Panzers*.
Poland, 1939.

foot 3, a very big guy. He had a submachine gun, and quickly figured out
what was taking place. He turned around, took the leader of the partisan
group, lifted him up with one hand and then dropped him down with his fist.
His men took us into custody, and we belonged to the Americans. The
sergeant then told the partisans to get away, and they did without hesita-
tion. By that time more vehicles and troops had arrived, so there was no
more argument.

Ever since that time I have had a tremendous respect and love for
black people. This man had saved the lives of nearly twenty German soldiers in our group. Without him I wouldn't be alive. God bless him. He was
humane. He did not care about our color, our uniform, that we were the
enemy; he knew what his objectives were and he carried them out. It was
zero hour for us. It was also the most heartwarming event I saw during my
entire service.

I will never forget when we got on trucks to go to the prison camp and
saw the American storage areas far back from the lines: trucks, dumps—
we couldn't believe our eyes what we saw—such materiel, superiority. We
scratched our heads and asked ourselves, how come it took them so long
to catch us? Even though it took a year and a half, it was essentially not
really a sustained war. For the most part it was a succession of more or
less minor battles, except of course Cassino and Anzio, and after a certain
time the Germans had decided to retreat. In a way, it was like the General
Sherman campaign to Atlanta in the American Civil War.

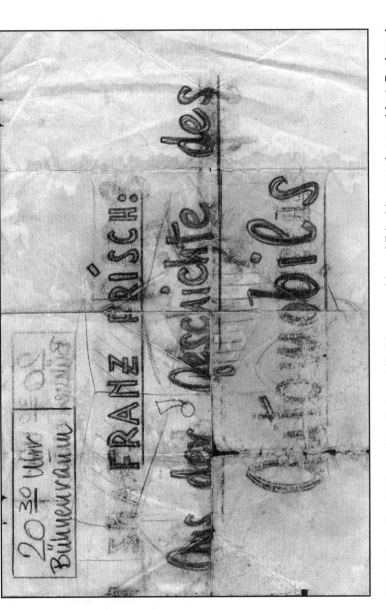

Titled "From the History of the Automobile," in recognition of Frisch's speech on subject. Designed by POW comrade Karl Filipsky of Vienna, "your friend," "In remembrance of the successful evening in the prison camp 339-4 in Pisa, Italy, 4 September 1946."

I was sent to a POW camp back in Pozzuoli outside of Naples, via a camp in between I can't remember. The boys had been separated from me. At that time there were about 300,000 German soldiers in captivity in Pozzuoli. We had problems with tents, problems with food, but I must say the Americans did their best. We were surprised to get anything. When we went into the camp at Pozzuoli we had big tents, and conditions were becoming tolerable. It beat sleeping in farmhouses and barnyards, and with the decent weather, erased some of my memories of Russian peasant houses in the snow.

The first half year in the POW camp was just subsistence. The Americans eventually provided us with the necessary food and clothing to stay alive and somewhat fit. After the first six months the Americans gradually became more organized, and even we prisoners were settled in—a vacation couldn't have been better. We heard over a loudspeaker in camp that Germany had surrendered, and later the Japanese, meaning the war was over now for everybody.

Nearby the camp was a big car manufacturing plant. We POWs were split up into teams of mechanics and worked some over there. I learned a lot about car repair. Months later in 1946 when I was at the next camp farther north, north of Rome, I was in charge of a vehicle repair shop for the Americans. Conditions by then were more relaxed, and familiarity

Frisch's column passes through damaged French city on the way into occupation following action at Dunkirk. Summer 1940.

Inside cover of German POW prayer book distributed by the Vatican. "Most earnestly we recommend our sons in the prisoners of war camps to the grace and pity and mercy of the Divine Saviour and we give them [the POWs] the divine blessing with all our heart as a sign of paternal love. Pius pp. XII....Words of blessing of the Holy Father, Pope Pius XII." Italy, 1946–47.

Suchet zuerst Gottes Reich und seine Gerechtigkeit, so wird Euch alles andere zufallen.

(Mt. 6, 33).

Ich weiss nicht, wohin mich Gott führt, aber das weiss ich, dass er mich führt.

(Gorch Fock).

IMPRIMATUR:

Die 31 augusti 1944.

† A. De Romanis, Ep. Porphyreonen., Vic. Gen. Civ. Vat.

GEBET DES KRIEGSGEFANGENEN.

O Gott, mein Schöpfer und Beschützer, ich weiss, Du bist mir nahe.

Ich verehre Dich und gebe mich Dir hin mit Leib und Seele und mit vollständiger Unterordnung unter Deinen hl. Willen. Du hast mich vom Tode errettet, der viele meiner Kameraden traf, während ich gefangen wurde. Aus Liebe zu Dir will ich alle Schwierigkeiten meiner Gefangenschaft geduldig und vertrauensvoll ertragen. Segne mich und alle meine Kameraden hier. Gewähre uns, in Frieden zu leben und uns

The POW prayer book. Quotations: "Search first for the Kingdom of God and His justice, and everything else will be yours. Matthew 6, 33." "I do not know where God is leading me, but I know that He leads me. Gorch Fock." "The Prayer of the Prisoner of War. Oh God, my Creator and Saviour, I know you are near to me. I admire you and with body and soul I will completely follow your holy plan. You have saved me from the death which hit many of my comrades when we went into captivity. Because of my love for you, I will take all difficulties of the captivity in full trust of you."

between Germans and our guards was accepted. I knew of no one who tried to escape, and one by one we were being discharged to go home.

The only depressing situation that arose was the concern of anybody who had family behind the Russian occupation zone, like me. Vienna, where my family was still living as far as I knew, was split four ways—same as Berlin. My address was in the American zone in Vienna, but Vienna was in the Russian occupation zone of Austria. Same situation as in East Germany. We who had relatives in the Russian zone had no news, no letters for one year, and we knew nothing about our families' fate during that time. I did write my family in Vienna from time to time to tell them my condition, but I never got a return letter. If I had thought to give as my home the address of my mother's sister in the American occupation zone—a person and place I could identify as my address—I would have been "home" one and a half years earlier. Because the Americans released prisoners with an American zone address first, or a British zone address, or French zone, they could go home. The last ones released lived in or behind the Russian zone.

I was in the POW camp in Italy for two years and did not get home until early May 1947. It did me no good to protest occasionally, for there was nothing the camp administrator could change, but it did give me and others like me some degree of understanding, and maybe sympathy and a few privileges as long as we behaved. I know of few German soldiers who failed to behave.

We had an interesting system in camp, and at the beginning for a long time we had our own guards. Living in the American prison camp after the first half year would today be considered a break from the real world, so to speak. We had good food, the weather was nice, we had absolutely nothing you could call bad treatment, and we practically had self-administration. We even used toilet paper and napkins for the first time in a long while, not for writing letters but for what it was intended. Toilet facilities and sanitary conditions were much improved. Sickness among soldiers went down. Plus we had car repair. Real luxuries for a man who had been mostly at the war front since September 1939. We received no pay, but what would we spend it on? Then all there was to do was sit and wait for release, a long wait for me, as I wondered so many times what I would find at home, and what the future would hold, once I was released. Pleasant conditions offset somewhat the drudgery and uncertainty of living from day to day as I was wondering when I would leave.

I was in Pozzuoli for longer than one year. I became good friends with a fellow who was much older than I, a lawyer, a sergeant, and after the war he was the secretary to Herr Fiegel, the *Bundeskanzler*, or chancellor, of Austria. Bundeskanzler Fiegel finalized the agreement between Russia and the United States to lift the occupation. My friend went home a little earlier than I because he had an American address. Through him I knew the *Bundeskanzler* quite well. I think Fiegel was the only one who could drink the Russians under the table. He was an agricultural engineer, his father had a large wine goods business, and he spoke fluent Russian, fluent English, fluent French. An extremely smart fellow.

All over the place there were a few thousand American trucks. The German guards and the American guards worked hand in hand to supply the Italian market with spare parts and tires, against the regulations of course. Looking back at the condition of Europe at the time, this kind of dealing was nothing unusual. We took advantage of whatever we were given. But slowly and surely the Americans wanted more and more of the profits, and the spare parts were gone, and then the deal was over. I know this because we had to transport the trucks to Livorno in order to be shipped back to the United States. I had a big truck with cranes, a lift truck, and when we picked up the cars only the cars in the first row had batteries and tires, and cars and trucks in the second row had no batteries and seldom had tires. Dealing in cars was one small way the Italian economy got re-started. It was just how we saw it at the time.

Cigarettes became the form of payments for preferred car repair service. If a guy wanted his car repaired quicker than those of others, he paid additionally in cigarettes. I started smoking in 1933 (I did not stop until 1999). Cigarettes were one of the most important and popular items in camp. I remember when we got to the first prison camp and were given a pack of Camels, American cigarettes, we just lay down and had one cigarette after another. We could not believe that luxury. I always got enough cigarettes, mostly American. We used "complete utilization of resources" and saved butts in metal boxes and had enough left over for rolling more cigarettes. We rolled our own, and used newspapers, toilet paper, anything. Always had enough toilet paper. At one place we got Italian tobacco, grown in Italy, which came in twenty-pound bags. We called it the "Italians' last revenge" (on us Germans). At first we couldn't smoke it because it was so damned strong. Then we washed it out with lemons to get the taste out, like making a tea, dried it, and then it was so wet it wouldn't burn. We needed at least three matches to light each cigarette. It was the most horrible tobacco I ever saw in my life. That's why we called it the "Italians' last revenge." But for those of us requiring the sustenance of tobacco, it might have been worth the struggle.

I considered my time in the prison camp as two years in the study of applied practical psychology. I learned one thing: The ones who survived the best were really simple farmers, smart, honest, intelligent people, with a solid but unsophisticated religious base, willing to take life as it is. They took it with grace. Those people survived mostly untouched. The ones with the biggest problems were the ones I call the half-intelligentsia: people who had studied a few semesters at the university, but not enough to understand what they had studied. They were the ones who knew enough to complain, who knew enough to philosophize, but they didn't know enough to accept their ignorance of most subjects. They almost mentally collapsed at first, and it was very hard for them to adjust to prison life. They knew a lot but understood nothing. They complained about how bad the world was and had no belief system. I found evaluating people very interesting.

Let me tell another story. It was at Christmas, 1945. We had one tent for the Catholic priest, and one tent for the Lutheran pastor. This Christmas Eve, suddenly there were hundreds of people in front of the tents. The Catholic priest said: "Those who were coming today just to find consolation, I don't need you. Will you be here tomorrow?" This was my first shock about the Catholic church, but it would not be my last. A few years later I became a Protestant and have been since.

Chapter 5

Ueber Kriegfuehren und zu Ueberleben Trachten
On Waging War and Waging Survival

Take the common street fighter as a comrade. If I go into battle with him, I know how he will shoot—at the enemy—and that he is reliable. But a higher class person as a comrade: I don't know whether he will shoot or not, but I know he doesn't want to be shot at. I had one comrade from home, a streetcar operator. He ran out of things to say after five minutes. But he was absolutely dependable in combat. It's fun to philosophize with a highly intelligent guy, but he might be utterly useless if your house gets flooded.

There were many times I feared for my life, but I never feared I would not make it through the war. I kept on and never gave up hope of going home alive because of prayers and letters from home, my own convictions, upbringing, and very firm constitution, and knowing I also had to keep my mouth shut.

Yes, I saw comrades shot. Some were killed. But a lot of my comrades survived the war. Those who survived the first battle had a greater chance of surviving the second battle than one who was new in the second battle. Those who survived the first half year or year had a much better chance of survival than the newcomers. Then if they survived the second combat the chances of survival got better and better. You got smarter, your instincts were sharper, what you would call the gut reaction was more relevant. I proved this theory would work, I suppose. I did survive campaigns and many, many battles in Poland, France, the Soviet Union, Sicily, and Italy. And the POW camp. I saw and experienced more than my share.

For example, you had a certain instinct, almost a nose for danger. We had a feeling of when to duck and when not to. We often came under counterbattery fire. We were very fast to move and take shelter and protect ourselves. It's amazing how quickly you can move if somebody shoots at you. For protection of sorts, most of the time we tried to dig a temporary

123

The reverse, or west, side of the famous Maginot Line between Germany and France. The *Panzers* did not assault the border fortress as the French had wished them to do, but instead outflanked the line and rendered it impotent, later capturing it. 1940.

At least the streets in this city have been cleared of enough rubble to allow vehicle columns to pass. France, 1940.

hole maybe one or one and one-half feet deep so we could just lie down. It can be done in a hurry. To have a cover is much more psychological than real. It is almost like the ostrich who puts his head in the sand. Obviously we preferred to stay in houses, barns, anything with a roof.

In 1958, my wife, children and I obtained visas to come to the United States and took permanent residence. We had an old Dodge, a marvelous car, and every weekend we drove out from New York into the country to see as much as we could. It took me a few years—at first I wasn't even aware of it—to overcome the urge to check the road ahead for the next place to hide in case someone started shooting. The need to look for cover was ingrained in me and took me years after the war to conquer. In order to learn this behavior, one has to live through a few experiences, as the chance for survival increased with the length of service.

In the German army, we *Soldaten* had a general unofficial doctrine that we had to fear our superior more than our enemy. Perhaps it was our training, such as U.S. Marines go through in boot camp. Besides our superiors, we had the eye and arm of the *SS,* the enforcers, to beware of at all times, and the so-called spy or informer who was probably in our unit somewhere. In all armies I think there is a different mentality, or morale, depending on whether you are on the march forward or on the march backward. Deep in enemy territory in Russia we were really not as much interested in defending the country if attacked. We were not giving up *our* country. We were giving up a part of the other guy's country. The closer the war came to German home territory the more vicious our defense became. The farther we moved away from home territory the weaker the defense got. Is this the nature of warfare always, or does it apply only to soldiers I knew once the war took a turn? One might argue that the German defenses at Cassino were not protecting our or the enemy's territory: it was like neutral ground, and keeping the enemy from getting any closer to our homeland in this case was important.

We had very few *Nazi* fanatics among our men—maybe one in a hundred. The true believers—maybe ten in one hundred. But the remaining men at first were just interested in getting their two-year service over and then going home one way or another. The two-year limit stopped as soon as the war started. Then it was for the duration or until they were dead or so badly wounded their usefulness at the front was nothing. Regardless of a few fanatics, a war is an experiment in survival and not an experiment in heroism.

This experience in survival is independent of color, social status, or education; it goes back to the most fundamental biological desire to survive. I love my children, parents, wife, whatever, but *I want to live.* It comes down to Masloff's hierarchy of needs at the lowest level, plus love, for a very restricted group of people. If we can accept this we devaluate all the

Infantrymen on bicycles pedal past Russian Orthodox church. 1941.

The flat Russian terrain provided little protection for a German rifleman. 1941.

German Mark II *Panzer* tank (PzKpfWII) heads for the front in France, 1940.

hero stories and to a large degree all ideologies. The crucial points are: One cannot live without an ideology and one cannot live with one, which may have a similarity to being married. For this I find no intelligent answers.

This statement may be somewhat trite, but some situations and events are awfully hard to describe for somebody who wasn't there, and I am almost amazed at the lack of understanding. American veterans have told me they also felt that other than historians and immediate families, the average person is not interested. I thought about this many times as I considered writing my memoir, and wondered what benefit it would bring. I have wondered, too, whether anyone holds any negative feelings toward me because I fought for Germany more than fifty years ago. Yes, I was one of Hitler's soldiers; this I cannot deny or change. But surely the warm, close, cooperative relations between West Germany and the United States as allies since 1945 must influence how someone views me and the minute role I played. This I must trust to be the case, and this feeling helped guide me into this memoir.

The war I fought in was the most destructive and most horrible of all time. I pray it will never be duplicated in any way for length, intensity, carnage, and damage. I decided to present my remembrances in hopes that someone would learn, someone would empathize, someone would be in a position to stop anything like it in the future. There is enough of a historian in me to realize that history can repeat itself, and that in general, humans do not absorb its lessons. I am not talking only to or about Germans, who started and lost two world wars this century. There are plenty of other examples I can use which will be understood.

Remember in the Vietnam War the incident of Lieutenant Calley and the My Lai massacre? Put yourself in that position as a German soldier in World War II. One motorcycle messenger doesn't come back, and we find him on the street with a slit throat. Next time we send through a truck with ten to twelve soldiers, and nothing happens. Then we lose another motorcycle messenger. We go into the village and all we find is a few old women and little children. I'm talking now about a partisan war or guerilla war. It was irrational. We faced this in many places, especially in France, Russia, and Italy. In the end you come to the point where you shoot at everything that moves and ask questions afterwards. I remember the reconnaissance by force one night in Russia. I don't know how many rounds we shot off in fear or reacting, but the next day we discovered we had hit a few animals. Still, it was preventive warfare: kill him before he kills me or one of my comrades.

Finally, a soldier doesn't act the way a civilian would consider rational. I don't ask: "Please identify yourself. Who are you?" I could give a shit who you are. I want to stay alive, and I shoot. I don't have to know what I shoot at. I think when Lieutenant Calley was convicted no one on the court had ever been in a partisan area or had experienced a guerilla war. I accept maybe Calley went crazy, but he wasn't a criminal. There is no such thing as a rational war, period, with people of rational behavior. It is a pipe dream regardless of how much operational research is done about a rational war. In the end what remains is that nobody wants to die. National goals and military objectives are fine, but in the end everybody wants to survive.[*]

I have always had a sense of humor. If I didn't have a sense of humor, I couldn't have lived through the war, or captivity, or the years right after the war either. If my group was together long enough I got to know the different individuals. Slowly and surely I knew to whom I could talk half decently, or express feelings to, and with whom to use caution. There were those few fanatics—they may not be bad people as human beings, but fanatics about the cause put them in a class alone, and with them I had to be extra careful.

I have no exact data but I would estimate that the number of deaths of men in my artillery units from battle actions were relatively low, definitely not more than fifteen percent. Most were from counterbattery fire, a few from tanks, a few from the air, very few from infantry. Probably only about another twenty percent were wounded, not bad for a German unit

---

[*] We faced a serious partisan threat in the Soviet Union, and to a lesser extent in Italy from the Communists, and at once hated them. Dealing with captured partisans was left up to the *SS*, who often ruthlessly tortured and killed them. I saw Russian partisans hanged. With us soldiers it often had to be shoot first and ask questions later. Hitler said, "This partisan war has its advantages. It gives us a chance to exterminate whoever opposes us." [Hitler in numerous sources]

Fresh snow-covered graves of Germans killed in the advance into the Soviet Union. Fall 1941.

that saw so much action. The biggest losses were in Russian prison camps. The Russian prison camps were, let's call it, murder. Understand why it was that way. To begin with, the Germans supposedly started the killing of prisoners and civilians because for one thing our leaders thought they were nearly subhuman (much less than Aryan-like Germans). If you are a Russian soldier and you barely have enough food for yourself, you may not be willing to give much food to the prisoners. However, if you are an American soldier and food comes out of your ears, you may be glad to give away low quality food to get rid of it.

War is atrocities. World War II was an atrocity in itself. War always is about property, either to gain the other person's property or to defend your own. Everything else is a smoke screen. But you need the smoke screen because if you tell the truth a lot of people wouldn't be willing to fight. I have learned not to make judgments: Those who are free of guilt, let them throw the first stone.

I never saw in Russia or elsewhere any human atrocities to soldiers or civilians. I did not capture any enemy or see any being captured. I did see hundreds of Polish, French, and Soviet army prisoners being sent to the rear, and, as I observed, they were always treated properly according to the rules of war. On the other hand, I did know a comrade captured at Stalingrad, a doctor, who died a few years after his release from prison

An announcement which got the Frenchman's attention: "Everybody who aids the English will be shot." 1940.

camp. He was "out of it—a vegetable" *[Frisch used here a slashing ges-ture across the head]* because of his experiences in captivity.

At the beginning of this remembrance when I began digging into my old material, I nearly had a panic attack. I wasn't willing to go through with it. When I finally managed to overcome this feeling, I was able to look to the past and then felt a relief. The panic attack, or shock, was like what we call in the United States the Vietnam syndrome. I think every soldier who goes through a war afterwards loses a part of himself, maybe a big piece. Something in him is destroyed, or not complete—I don't know what I should call it. The big difference, and it is big, is when we German soldiers went home after the prison camp in 1947, and those who had come home earlier, we simply had no time to be aware of my syndrome. We had no time to sit in self-pity and feel sorry for ourselves or our generation. We had to do whatever was necessary to stay alive.

Our homelands were partially or totally destroyed. We went to the farmers to trade old family pieces, a golden ring, a watch, whatever it was, for potatoes, a few eggs. We wanted to, we tried, to keep living. Under conditions like this you don't think back, you only think ahead and how to survive the next day, how to survive, how to make it—you look forward. You accept tacitly that the zero hour is over, and that it can only get better, regardless of what the future brings.

I think every soldier is capable of having similar experiences. When we are on the front line we do not philosophize, do not discuss the value of the world, the value of mankind. Occasionally we prayed, sometimes quite a lot, but we did not engage in essentially useless chatter about nothing, or march in protest. If my stomach is full, I have warm clothes for winter, and in the summer an air conditioner, then I am able to think of many ideas of how to improve the world, what to do—only then. Let's face it, the hierarchy of Masloff, the triangle, starts with survival. At the top is self-satisfaction or self-fulfillment, as it is called. I am not dreaming. I always tell my students, if I am a forward artillery observer, and the enemy tank is coming, I either run, or hide, or shoot, but I definitely don't make a study.

Today we have pictures showing the civilian population as they started their trek back to Germany from Russia. All those pictures were accurate, but there was a psychological development of the breakthrough that is always ignored in history. The French historian Fernadel Brodel, who wrote of the history of the daily life of the population (1600–1700), was the first writer who even made an attempt to talk about the daily life. We read in history of things you could see—big battles. We talk about big battles, ethnic cleansing, and all those things. Do we really understand how people feel, what it means to have fear, what it means for a mother to cry for her child? This is what makes life. We are always somebody on cloud nine, and we really ignore life. In all our histories we are talking about the beautiful victories. We should talk more about beautiful lives.

The regiment's Christmas party, 1940, in France. Frisch is standing at the rear on left by tree. Next to him is Private Karl Filipsky, who wrote the "History of the car" certificate when they were both POWs in Italy in 1945 (see certificate p. 117). The officers mixed with enlisted men at parties.

Curious German soldiers examine downed French Potez 74.1 reconnaissance aircraft. France, 1940.

Frisch, *second from left*, and comrades enjoy rowing on a French lake in the Loire Valley. Summer 1940.

At the 1940 Christmas party in France, caricatures spoof regimental life: "I am the ghost of Izdebnik," a Polish village where their 8cm gun was destroyed. Inscribed on the back: "As Casanova he was well known, has a bride in every country. He speaks with great flamboyance about Poland—however, those who were there do not believe him."

For the first time in modern history, at least in the German language, an Austrian baroness talked about her experience in war. She wrote about the war between Prussia and Austria from the human side, the side of my mother. In the battles and victories, you can identify the general who won, you can identify the general who lost; afterwards you find a hundred reasons why someone won or lost. Who mentions today the twenty million people who got shot under Stalin, the twenty million people who lost their lives in the *gulags* under Stalin? Who talks today about the thousands of dead children in the holy wars, and the Crusade? Nobody. They were what we termed in World War I as "cannon fodder." People's lives have been reduced to a number, a statistic. Now I realize that when we venture into this area, we may lose any belief of human progress. Very sorry. Sometimes I have the feeling we are at the same level with the cannibals, only we found out that human meat is not good enough to eat.

I couldn't help but feel and understand the meanings of these concepts. I had no desire to be part of a grand design for conquest. All I wanted was to do my job for my country and get the war over with, like the rest of my comrades. I was not a *Nazi* nor did I want to be. In fact, my political leanings were the other way, as I described in the opening of this memoir. I was a young man of nineteen, not long out of *Gymnasium*. I didn't ask to go into military life, and certainly not to go to war. I had no choice—the draft is the same in every country, but under the *Nazis* it was a bit tougher to avoid. I had thoughts and hopes for the future as an engineer.

Maybe the artillery soldier Franz Frisch had it somewhat easier than the foot soldier, or the aviator, or the tank driver: I didn't have to see the results of my work, the shell that landed twenty kilometers away, and count the numbers of dead, whether soldiers or civilians. As we advanced, I couldn't tell if it was *my* battery, or *my* cannon, which had destroyed the farmhouse we were passing, or killed the family pet. Artillery work for the most part is very impersonal. This was never lost on us. For me, the war had moments when it too was impersonal. Such is called insensitivity.

———

In July 1934, the family was spending our summer vacation in Karintia, on a lake, where my mother's brother had a summer home. Here we got the message of the murder of the Austrian Christian fascist Chancellor Engelbert Dollfuss by *Nazis*. Local militia formed units to defend Austria against an expected German invasion. Mussolini protected Austria, but the smell of war was in the air. It was a frightful week.

I also remember well the day March 12, 1938, when my mother cried. It was the first time, since my father, her husband, died in 1929. Hitler appeared in triumphant parade through the streets of Vienna. Unification had happened. I still hear her words: "Now we lost *unsere Heimat* [our

Advancing columns pass disabled French heavy Char B1bis tank. 1940.

German infantry proceed on bicycles. France, 1940.

homeland]." My mother had strong ties to the old Austria, and a unification with Germany was unimaginable to her. Our freedoms were gone.

I am today most concerned about the potential danger we Americans face in losing our freedoms. Look at General Colin Powell several years ago, as an example. He was invited to speak at Harvard University. People protested his position on gays and lesbians in the military and interrupted him without respect for him or his position. If we continue this way, in the end nobody will be allowed to speak anymore in public, for everybody offends somebody. One guy may be too religious, the other may be too liberal for some. You name it. "Political correctness," as it is called, will curtail free speech, free thought, free expression, leaving it up to the state to decide in court or administrative judgment whether the First Amendment rights no longer apply. It means we may reach the point where we say, "Yes, sir. *Heil Hitler.*" And this is what makes my spine tingle—I have been through this. Now the good thing is we in the United States don't have one unified force, a universal political philosophy, as we had under Hitler and the *Nazis.* Maybe this lack of uniformity will avoid a catastrophe. I hope so.

This is something the American tells me he simply cannot understand—what it means to live in an absolute dictatorship as we had under Hitler, and even worse under Stalin. You are not free to speak or free to act. And every word you speak can be turned against you by somebody. If you say in the United States the president is a fool, your friend may look at you, he may agree with you, or he may say, "Come on. Don't say such bullshit." In an absolute dictatorship, every person lives for himself. Nobody gets involved in political discussions. Parents are afraid to talk freely in front of their children. The teacher might get the message. All attention, actions, and interests, are oriented toward *survival!* Rationality is eliminated. The world becomes self-centered and rotates around the family.

I will share a story. I had a very good friend, a 100-percent honest fellow. He didn't make it back from Stalingrad. We were staying together in a little hotel room after the campaign in France. One day we were talking and he told me, "Franz, if you say this once more I will have to report you." We were good friends, but he was a 150-percent believer in the *Nazi* cause. This is what the Americans cannot understand. If the American would understand, he would realize that freedom is not a right—freedom is a privilege. It is a privilege that we have to preserve, and we have to earn it every day.

The book has never been written on how the screw was turned slowly and surely till all freedom was gone. Government, centralized or not, can grow until it has the power to take what you have. This is what I fear. A book like this doesn't have glorious stories to tell—there were no glorious stories. I saw it happen like this: The little teacher educating the children about freedom and working in a school close to home just was transferred to a school two hours away. The teacher wasn't interested in traveling two hours in the morning and in the evening in a railroad car. So he stopped

The local peasants were not afraid of their invaders. Russia, Summer 1941.

140

Overturned French farmer's cart with its fallen horses, victims of aircraft strafing. 1940.

Russian peasants gather for a burial. 1941.

October 1941, during the drive for Moscow. Moscow is to the right, 49 km; go straight for Gshatsk; Bark Kamp is 7 km ahead; IDF (German units) are to the right; Wjasma and a field hospital are to the left. Mud, however, is everywhere.

World War I French soldiers' cemetery. Commenting on the damaged cross: "If they are killed twice they are definitely dead," Frisch remembers the men saying. 1940.

Frisch, *center*, and friends prepare to enjoy a French café meal with plates, glasses, and silverware. "We tried to be cultivated. It was beautiful." France, late 1940.

talking about freedom. This mustn't happen to him. It was just a warning, a message, which was understood by all.

Suddenly parents were afraid to talk in front of their children. The children might say stupid things to their friends, and then their parents could have reported them. This is why I am so against—I hope it not misunderstood—politically correct speech. I am becoming wary of this term. It reminds me so much of the time when we had to know what represented politically correct or politically incorrect speech, and how it would affect our very life.

When I went home to Vienna from the POW camp in May 1947, I realized the whole world had completely changed. There was suddenly on a Sunday an announcement in the newspaper that the German mark was being changed to the new Austrian schilling. We could take our identification booklet, which everybody had to have with a photo, to the bank and withdraw 100 new schillings from our savings account, regardless of what we had deposited in the account. I had approximately 10,000 old marks in my savings account, a considerable amount. I got only 100 schillings and a stamp in my savings book and on my identification booklet: "Money exchanged." Suddenly everybody started a new era with 100 schillings.

My mother was a teacher. There was a uniform salary of 100 schillings for a few months for every government employee, and then the salary started to differentiate. The schilling had been the Austrian currency before the unification. Overnight the black market disappeared because the black market had lost all its money and had no way to exchange it; the currency had become useless. At that time the economy started to pick up. We were very reluctant in the Russian zone to do anything, because we were afraid of getting expropriated or occupied by a new Russian unit. Nobody painted their houses. The West, including West Germany, started to recover economically. Life was a flower there.

When we former soldiers went to the university after prison camp we were classified as *Spaet-Heimkehrer*, which means late homecomer. There we had certain privileges in selecting courses, with no payment at all. They were approximately the kind of privileges the soldiers had in the United States, like a G.I. Bill. Cost us nothing. And our freedoms were back.

My old artillery units held a few reunions, *Treffen*, in Vienna, but I lost contact with them after I left to live in the United States in 1958. I doubt there were more than two hundred men out of hundreds who survived. Most losses occurred from the part of the unit that was detached and sent to Stalingrad, and many of the others ended up sunk on the way to the *Afrika Korps*.

I had a friend in Vienna I went through *Gymnasium* with, and last talked with him in 1991. He is Jewish but converted to Episcopalian. My family hid him in our house during the war until he could escape to Switzerland and regain his freedom. He is a retired vice president of Kaiser Aluminum. He got sick and I really needed to call him. It was, it is, never too late.

Chapter 6

Franz Frisch, die Nachkriegsjahre
Franz Frisch, the Post-War Years

Franz A. P. Frisch resumed his education at the Technical University of Vienna in 1947. He received his bachelor of mechanical engineering degree in 1950, his *Diplom-Ingenieur* (master of science) as a Professional engineer in naval architecture and marine engineering in 1952, and his *Doktor der Technischen Wissenschaft* (doctor of technical sciences) in 1971, all from the Technical University of Vienna.

After beginning his career in marine and shipyard engineering on the Danube River, within the Russian-occupied zone, he moved to Hamburg, Germany in 1951 to work for the Howaldtwerke Hamburg (HWH) shipyard, one of the nation's largest. He progressed through management levels and succeeded as head of the department of shipyard maintenance and planning. In 1956, the U.S. Maritime Administration invited him to testify on European shipbuilding technology and costs. This established his international credentials as a naval architect and consultant.

Later, in 1958, he, his wife, and children immigrated to the United States. He became associated with several naval architect firms in New York City and Washington, D.C. on projects primarily for the Maritime Administration, and with shipyards and companies in Brazil, Japan, and Europe.

In 1963, he joined the Center for Naval Analyses in Alexandria, Virginia, as a consultant and scientific advisor to the U.S. Naval Sea Systems Command's (NAVSEA) PM-10 program management office, the LHA amphibious assault ship and AGC amphibious command ship project offices, and to other navy projects where he utilized his education and experience in marine engineering and naval architecture. He developed the plans for the new FDL fast logistics ship.

From 1968 to 1974, he taught marine engineering and engineering management at the Massachusetts Institute of Technology, and consulted on shipyard projects in Dubai. He has subsequently taught at Virginia Tech and Central Michigan University.

Frisch with his mother, Margarete, at the *Gasthaus Bauer*. Margarete's sister owned the inn in the Forstau bei Steyr, Upper Austria. Circa 1948.

He joined the technical staff of NAVSEA in Arlington, Virginia, in 1973, serving until he joined the faculty of the Defense Systems Management College (DSMC) in 1978 as a professor of engineering management. He later became director of the Technical Management Department. He returned to NAVSEA to work in the commander's office in 1980, and in 1987 returned to the faculty at DSMC. He is one of a handful of persons to be awarded the title professor emeritus by DSMC. At DSMC, a principal Department of Defense school teaching graduate-level courses in defense acquisition management, he was a professor of engineering management and taught, mentored students, and directed various research projects in defense acquisition management.

Dr. Frisch has been married to the former Gertrude (Traudel) Schreiner of Vienna for more than 45 years. They have three daughters and two grandchildren. Until his retirement in June 1998 and move to Jackson, Mississippi, they resided in Alexandria, Virginia.

Selected Bibliography
for Further Recommended Reading

Anders, Wladyslaw. *Hitler's Defeat in Russia*. Chicago: Henry Regnery Co., 1953.

Bethell, Nicholas. *The War Hitler Won: The Fall of Poland*. September 1939. New York: Holt, Rinehart and Winston, 1972.

Bethell, Nicholas, and the editors of Time-Life Books. *Russia Besieged*. Alexandria, Va.: Time-Life Books, 1977.

Cecil, Robert, ed., consultant, and Simon Goodenough, ed. *Hitler's War Machine*. London: Salamander Books, Ltd., 1996.

Chapman, Guy. *Why France Fell: The Defeat of the French Army in 1940*. New York: Holt, Rinehart and Winston, 1968.

Collier, Richard. *The Sands of Dunkirk*. New York: E. P. Dutton & Co., Inc., 1961.

Cooper, Matthew. *The German Army 1933–1945: Its Political and Military Failure*. U.S.A.: Stein and Day Publishers, 1978.

Dollinger, Hans. *The Decline and Fall of Nazi Germany and Imperial Japan: A Pictorial History of the Final Days of World War II*. New York: Gramercy Books, 1995.

Dupuy, T. N., and Paul Martell. *Great Battles on the Eastern Front: The Soviet-German War, 1941–1945*. Indianapolis: Bobbs-Merrill Co., 1982.

Fleming, Peter. *Invasion 1940: An Account of the German Preparations and the British Countermeasures*. London: Rupert Hart-Davis, 1957.

Gilbert, Martin. *The Day the War Ended: May 8, 1945; Victory in Europe*. New York: Henry Holt and Co., 1995.

Goerlitz, Walter. *History of the German General Staff, 1757–1945*. New York: Frederick A. Praeger, Inc., 1959.

Griess, Thomas E., ed. *Atlas of the Second World War: Europe and the Mediterranean*. Wayne, N.J.: Avery Publishing Group, The West Point Military History Series, n.d.

Guderian, Heinz. *Panzer Leader.* New York: Ballantine Books, 1957.

Hart, B. H. Liddell. *The German Generals Talk: Startling Revelations from Hitler's High Command.* New York: Quill, 1979.

Hogg, Ian V. *German Artillery of World War Two.* London: Greenhill Books; and Mechanicsburg, Pa.: Stackpole Books, 1997.

Horne, Alistair. *To Lose a Battle: France 1940.* Boston: Little, Brown and Co., 1969.

Jackson, W. G. F. *The Battle for Italy.* New York: Harper & Row, 1967.

Keegan, John, ed. *Atlas of the Second World War.* London: Geographia, 1996.

Kemp, Anthony. *The Maginot Line: Myth and Reality.* New York: Stein and Day, 1982.

Laffin, John. *Jackboot: A History of the German Soldier, 1713–1945.* New York: Barnes & Noble, Inc., 1995.

Leach, Barry A. *German Strategy Against Russia, 1939–1941.* Oxford: Clarendon Press, 1973.

Linklater, Eric. *The Campaign in Italy. The Second World War, 1939–1945.* London: His Majesty's Stationery Office, 1951.

Mondey, David. *Axis Aircraft of World War II.* London: Chancellor Press, 1996.

Nafziger, George F. *The German Order of Battle: Panzers and Artillery in World War II.* London: Greenhill Books; and Mechanicsburg, Pa.: Stackpole Books, 1999.

Pimlott, John. *The Historical Atlas of World War II.* New York: Henry Holt and Co., 1995.

Pond, Hugh. *Salerno.* Boston: Little, Brown and Co., 1961.

Ransford, Simon, ed. *War Machines: Land.* London: Octopus Books, 1975.

Rothbrust, Florian K. *Guderian's XIXth Panzer Corps and the Battle of France: Breakthrough on the Ardennes.* Westport, Conn.: Praeger, 1990.

Salisbury, Harrison E. *The Unknown War.* New York: Bantam Books, 1978.

Seaton, Albert. *The Russo-German War 1941–45.* New York: Praeger Publishers, 1971.

Shepperd, G. A. *The Italian Campaign 1943–45: A Political and Military Re-assessment.* New York: Frederick A. Praeger Publishers, 1968.

Shirer, William L. *The Rise and Fall of the Third Reich: A History of Nazi Germany.* New York: Simon and Schuster, 1960.

Speer, Albert. *Inside the Third Reich.* New York: The Macmillan Co., 1970.

Tessin, G. West German Government Publication. Vol. 6.

Tregaskis, Richard. *Invasion Diary.* New York: Random House, 1944.

Tsouras, Peter G. *Fighting in Hell: The German Ordeal on the Eastern Front.* London: Greenhill Books; and Mechanicsburg, Pa.: Stackpole Books, 1995.

Vannoy, Allyn R., and Jay Karamales. *Against the Panzers: United States Infantry Versus German Tanks, 1944–1945.* Jefferson, N.C.: McFarland & Co., Inc., 1996.

Veranov, Michael, ed. *The Mammoth Book of the Third Reich at War.* New York: Carroll & Graf Publishers, Inc., 1997.

Wallace, Robert, and the editors of Time-Life Books. *The Italian Campaign.* Alexandria, Va.: Time-Life Books, 1978.

Wernick, Robert, and the editors of Time-Life Books. *Blitzkrieg.* New York: Time-Life Books, 1976.

Westwood, J. D. *Eastern Front: The Soviet-German War 1941–45.* Greenwich, Conn. Bison Books Corp., 1984.

Williamson, Gordon. *Loyalty is My Honor: Personal Accounts from the Waffen-SS.* Osceola, Wisc.: Motorbooks International, 1995.

Wray, Timothy A. *Standing Fast: German Defensive Doctrine on the Russian Front During World War II; Prewar to March 1943.* Fort Leavenworth, Kans.: U.S. Army Command and General Staff College, 1986.

Ziemke, Earl F. *Army Historical Series: Stalingrad to Berlin: The German Defeat in the East.* Washington: Center of Military History, United States Army, 1987.

Ziemke, Earl F., and Magna E. Bauer. *Moscow to Stalingrad: Decision in the East.* Army Historical Series. Washington: Center of Military History, U.S. Army, 1987.

Index

Photographs in italics.

A

Africa(n) duty, xxxvii, 17
Allies (Allied forces), xxx–xxxii, 10, 19, 35,
    51, 58, 104, 108–10, 112, 114
American(s). *See also* United States.
  country, xix, 110, 120, 138
  force(s), xv, xvii, xxiv, xxxii, 11, 104, 106,
    114, 118, 120, 121
  soldier(s), 5, 29, 37, 100
Anschluss, xv, xxxi, 2, 37
Apennine Mountains (Northern Apennines),
    Italy, 107, 110
Asia, xxx
Atlantic Ocean, xxx, 58
Australia, xxxi
Austria, xix, xxxi, xxxii, 2, 5, 10, 13, 22, 37,
    102, 110, 114, 120, 136, 138
  Austrian Occupation Zones
    American, 120
    British, 120
    French, 120
    Russian, 144, 145
  places
    Forstau bei Steyr, *146*
    Gasthaus Bauer, *146*
    Karintia, 136
    National Museum of Art, 102
    St. Stefan's Cathedral, Vienna, 11, 12
    Steyr (city), 13, 63
    Technical University of Vienna, 17, 96,
      103, 145
    Upper Austria, *146*
  Viennese, 4, 10, 32
Austrian Government
  Christian-Austrian Faciscm, 1
  Dollfuss, Engelbert, 1, 5, 136
  Fiegel, Chancellor, 120
  Hapsburg, 1
  Hapsburg Palace, 37
  Schuschnigg, Kurt von, 1

B

Berlin, Germany, xxxii, xxxiii, 95, 120
Bonn, Germany, 37
Braun, Wernher von, xix
Brazil, 145
Britain, xxx, xxxi, 47, 60
  British army (forces), xxxii, 29, 51, 56,
    58, 104, 112
    Eighth Army, 106, 109
    Montgomery, Sir Bernard, 106
Brodel, Fernadel, 132
Brossier, Marcel, *57*

C

Casanova, *135*
Center for Naval Analyses, Alexandria,
    Va., 145
Central Michigan University, Mount
    Pleasant, Mich., 145
Churchill, Winston, 109
Cold War, The, 97
Crusade, The, 136
Czar, 78, 94
Czechoslovakia, xxxi, xxxii, 8, 11, 29, 32,
    51, 96
  Bohemia, 32
  Brno, 11, 32
  Carpathian Mountains, 51
  Prague, 32
  Sudetenland, xxxi

D

Defense Systems Management College,
    Alexandria, Va., xiv, xv, 146

Department of Defense (U.S.), 146
Depression, Great, xxx
Dubai, 145
Dulles, Allen, 22, 110

E

Eastern Front (East). *See* Soviet Union/
    Russia, Campaign in
East Germany, 120
England, xxxi, 98. *See also* Britain
English Channel, xix, xxxi, xxxii, 51, 56, 58
Europe, xiv, xxx, xxxi, 37, 51, 104, 121, 145
  Central Europe, 87
  Western Europe, xxxi
European War (not Frisch's)
  Ardennes Forest (offensive), xxxii, xxxiv,
      xxxvi, 51
  Battle of the Bulge, xxxii
  Belgium/Belgian, xxxi, 51, 98
  Denmark, xxxi
  Low Countries, 51
  Luxembourg, xxxi, 51
  Netherlands, xxxi
  Normandy, xxxii
  Norway, xxxi
  Operation Sea Lion, 60
  "Phoney War," xxxi, 51
  Remagen, xxxii
  Siegfried Line (Westwall), xxxii, 51
  VE-Day, xxxiii
  Western Front, xxxii, 74

F

France *(Frankreich)*, Campaign in, 1940
    (Frisch's)
  battles
    Dunkirk, xxxi, 10, 56, 58–60
    Montreuil S.M., 56
    Sedan, xxvi, 56, 58
  invasion of, and Battle of, xvii, xxiv, xxxi,
      xxxiv, xxxvi, xxxvii, 2, 10, 17, 46,
      103, *113*, 138
  France
    country (national), xxii, xxiii, xxx–xxxii,
        xxxvi, 17, 29, 31, 32, 46, 47, 51,
        53, 60, 64, 78, 91, 104, 112, 118,
        123, 132, 134, 143
    French forces, 43, 51, 56, 58, 111
    French soldiers, xix, *xlii, 33, 40, 51, 57,
        59, 61, 142*
    in photographs, *xxvi, xxvii, xxxvi, 4, 6,
        7, 9, 12, 14, 16, 17, 20, 21, 39, 40,
        42, 43, 53, 55–58, 61–67, 111, 118,
        124, 128, 133, 134*
  places
    Abbeville, 58
    Amiens, 58
    Bastogne (Belgium), 56
    Boulogne, 58
    Calais, xxxi, 56, 58
    "Hotel du October," 58
    La Neuville aux Jogtes, *18*
    Loire Valley, 60, *134*
    Maginot Line, xix, 51, 56, 58, 60, *111, 124*
    Marcel's "Grand Garage," *xxvii*
    Montcomet, 56
    Peronne, 58
    Rheims, 32, 56, 60, *62, 65*, 101
    Stonne, 58
    St. Quentin, 56, 58
    Versailles, Palace of, 66
    Vichy (government), 60
  French Military Equipment
    Char B1bis tank, *137*
    Potez 74.1 aircraft, *134*
  Frisch, Franz A. P.
    as coauthor, xxvii, 132
    pre-war, *xx*, 1, 2, *3*, 37
    as German simple soldier, xiv, xix, xxi,
        xxv, 136
    administration/training, xvii, xxxvi, xxxvii,
        36, *101, 113*
    campaign in France, xxiii, *4*, 6, 16, *21*,
        42, *56, 57*, 62, *64*, 65, 66, *67*, 118,
        133, 134, 138, *143*
    campaign in Italy, 102, *109*
    campaign in Poland, 23, 34, *52*
    campaign in Sicily, 106
    campaign in Soviet Union (Russia),
        xviii, xxvix, 13, *16*, 36, 72, *76, 80*,
        81, 82, 91, 97
    as prisoner of war, 117
    post-war, xiv, xv, *xx,* xxvii, 38, 145, 146,
        148
  Frisch, Franz Xaver, 1
  Frisch, Margarete (Paradeiser), 1, *3, 146*
  Fock, Gorch, 119

G

German Army. *See Wehrmacht*
German forces. *See Wehrmacht*
German soldiers. *See Wehrmacht*
Germany, xvii, xxxi, xxxii, 17, 19, 22, 29,
    37, 46, 51, 88, 96, 110–12, 114,
    118, 128, 132, 138
German (Germanic), xix, xxii, xxvii, xxx,
    10, 29, 35, 46, 58, 60, 85, 96, 112,
    119, 125, 143
  in photographs, *101, 113*
  language, xxii, 136
  places
    Bavaria(n), xxxii, 10, 103

Eifel Region, 51
Frankfurt, xxxii
Hamburg, 145
Hermesdorf bei Waldbroil, *113*
Howaldtwerke Hamburg shipyard, 145
Koeln (Cologne), 51, 103, 113
Mainz, xxxii
Munich, 111
Osnabrueck, 100
Rhineland, xxxi, 103
Southern Germany, xxxii
Western Germany, xxxi
German Government and Politics
　Himmler, Heinrich, xxxiii
　Hindenburg, Paul von, xxx
　organizations
　　Axis, xxxii, 104
　　Gestapo, 32, 111
　　Hitler Youth, xxxvi
　　Nazis (*Nazi* Party), xxx, xxiv, 27, 37, 41,
　　　112, 125, 136, 138
　　　treatment of European Jews, xxvii
　　SA, 32
　　SS, xxxiii, 22, 32, 37, 111, 125, 129
　　Waffen-SS, xxxiii
　Reich, xxx
　Reich, Third, xxiv, xxxi
Gestapo. See German Government and
　　Politics
G.I. Bill, 144
G.I. Joe/Willie and Joe (U.S.), xxii, 5

H

Haas, Lieutenant, 109
Harvard University, Cambridge, Mass.,
　138
Heer, das (German Army). *See Wehrmacht*
Hirsch, Edward, xiv
Hitler, Adolf, xxii, xxx, xxxiii, 2, 37, 129. *See
　also* German Government and
　Politics
　as commander in chief, xix, xxiv, xxxi, 19,
　　58, 60, 78, 86, 110, 128
　as *Fuehrer*, 41, 46, 58, 85, 138
Holocaust, The, xxvii

I

Italy *(Italien)*, Campaign in, 1943–45
　　(Frisch's)
　also, Defense of, xvii, xxiv, 2, 100, 102
　battles and campaigns
　　Anzio, 108, 116
　　Cassino (Montecassino), 78, 108, 109,
　　　116, 125
　　Gothic Line, 17, 110, 112
　　Gustav Line, 108, 109

Northern Italy, 22
Salerno, xxxii, 102, 108
country, xxxii, 4, 10, 17, 22, 24, 29, 31,
　34, 46, 102–4, 106, 108, 110, 112,
　117, 123, 129, 133
Italian Front, 35
Neapolitan, 103
in photographs, *102, 109*
places
　Adriatic Sea, 110
　Agropoli, 108
　Alps, 110, 114
　Amalfi, 108
　Arezzo, 110
　Bay of Naples, 108
　Bologna, 110, 114
　Calabria (Reggio Calabria), xxxii, 108
　Capri, 102
　Carrara, 110
　Caserta, 108
　Florence, 110
　Formia, 109
　Gaeta, 109
　Gulf of Salerno, 108
　Lake Garda, 110
　Liri River Valley, 108
　Livorno, 121
　Northern Italy, 112
　Ostiglia, 110, 112, 114
　Pesaro, 110
　Pisa, 110, 117
　Poggio Berni, *109*
　Pompei, 102
　Pozzuoli, 101, 110, 118, 120
　Rome, 109, 118
　Southern Italy, 108
　South Tirol,
　Tirol, 114
　San Marino, 110

J

Jackson, Miss., xxvii, 146
Japan, 145
Jones, Wilbur D., Jr. (coauthor), xx, xxi,
　xxii, 4, 5, 38

K

Kaiser Aluminum, 144
Kalegi, Coudenhove, 1
Kodak, xix, *xx*, xxi, 5, 37

L

Lili Marlene, 47

M

Mack, Kapitaen, *105*

Maddox, Richard, xx
Marines. *See* U.S. Marines
Maritime Administration (U.S.), 145
Masloff, 125, 132
Massachusetts Institute of Technology,
    Cambridge, Mass., 145
Mauldin, Bill, xxii
Mediterranean Sea, xxvii, xxx, 100, 103, 104
Michigan, Upper Peninsula of, xix, 5
Morgenthau Plan, 111, 112
Morgenthau, Henry, 112
Mussolini, *Il Duce* Benito (Italy), 112, 136

N

Naples, Italy, 17, 100, 101, *102*, 108, 110,
    118
Napoleon Bonaparte, 78
Naval Sea Systems Command (NAVSEA)
    (U.S.), 145, 146
Navy, U.S. *See* U.S. Navy
Nazis. See German Government and
    Politics
New York
  city, 145
  state, 125
New Zealand, xxxi
North Africa(n) Campaign, xxi, 103, 104
  desert, 100
  Tunis, xxi, 103
North Pacific, xiv
North Pole, 41

P

Pacific Ocean, xxx
Paris, France, xxxi, *19*, 56, 60, *64–66*
  Eiffel Tower, 60, *65*
  Sacre Coeur, *65*
Peoples
  Austrians, 11, 12, 32, 37, 136, 143
  Czechoslovakians (Czechs), 32
  Europeans, 15, 86, 145
  French, *61*, 131, 140
  Germans, xxx, xxxi, 37, 128
  Hungarians, 1
  Italians, 112, 121
    partisans, 114, 115
  Moroccans, *xlii*
  Poles, *23*, 47, *48, 50*
  Rumanians, xxxii
  Sicilians, 104, 112
  Soviets (Russians), *70, 80, 89, 94*, 121,
    139, 140
Pius XII, Pope (Holy Father), 119
Poland *(Polen)*, Campaign in, 1939
    (Frisch's)
  British-French ultimatum, 47, 98

invasion of, xvii, xxiv, xxxvii, 2, 8, 10, 46,
    51
  in photographs, xxxv, *xlii, 2, 8, 23, 25, 34,
    47–50, 115, 116, 135*
  Poland/Polish (country, national), xxxi,
    xxxii, xxxvi, 29, 31, 37, 47, 51, 52,
    56, 60, 69, 78, 98, 123
  Polish forces, 46, *50*
  Polish soldiers, xix, *47, 49*
  places
    Czestochowa, 46
    Izdebnik, 135
    Posen, 47, *48*
Powell, Colin, 138
Prussia, 136

R

Red Army (Soviet Union). *See* Soviet
    Union/Russia, Campaign in
Reich, Third. *See* German Government
    and Politics
Rivers
  Bug, 51, 69, 73
  Danube, 145
  Garigliano, 108
  Meuse, 58
  Po (Po River Valley), xxxii, 110, 112
  Rapido, 108
  Rhine, xxxii
  Somme, 58
  Volturno, 108
Russia. *See* Soviet Union/Russia,
    Campaign in

S

Schreiner (Frisch), Gertrude (Traudel), 146
Sicily *(Sizilien)*, Campaign in, 1942–43
    (Frisch's)
  also, Defense of, xvii, xxiv, 2, 100
  Italian army in Sicily, 104, 106
    Guzzoni, Alfredo, 104
    Sixth Army, 104
Sicily, xxxii, 4, 11, 17, 31, 103, 104, *105,
    106*, 123
  places
    Bagheria, 106
    Castelveltrano, 104
    Catania, 104
    Gulf of Gela, 104
    Licata, 104
    Marsala, 104
    Mazzara Mountains, 106
    Messina, xxxii, 104, 106, 108
    Palermo, xxi
    Syracuse, 104

Termini, 106
Trapani-Marsala, 104
Tyrrhenian Sea (Coast), 106
Soldiers, German. *See Wehrmacht*
Soviet Union/Russia *(Sowjetunion/
    Russland)* (USSR), Campaign in,
    1941 (Frisch's)
battles and campaigns
    Barantino, 73
    Bryansk, 73
    Bryansk-Vyazma, 84, 108
    Byelorussia, 2, *12*, 69, *77*, *88*
    Eastern Front (East), xxxii, xxxiii, 19,
        82, 85, 96
    Minsk, *xviii*, 73, 74
    Moscow, xix, xxxii, *xliii*, 10, 15, 17, 19,
        35, 73, 74, 78, 82, 84–86, 95, 96,
        98, 108, *141*
    Operation *Barbarossa,* 69
    Operation *Taifun,* 82
    Orsha, 73
    Russian Front, xiv, 8, 35, 85
    Smolensk, *16*, 24, *25*, 32, 73, 74, *75*,
        77, 82–84, 92, 108
    Stalingrad, xvii, xxxii, 11, 20, 21, 24, 27,
        35, 78, 96, 100, 103, 138
    Vyazma, 84, 108
    Yelnya (Jelna) Line, 24, *25*, 32, 73, 75,
        77, 78, 83
    Yelna-Desna River salient, 74
invasion of, xxiv, xxxvii, 2, 10, 17, 24, 29,
    31, 38, 51, 69
places
    Bark Kamp, *141*
    Brest-Litovsk (Poland), 69, 73
    Caucasus, xxxii
    European Russia, 85
    Gshatsk, *141*
    Kaluga, 84
    Kursk, xxxii
    Obininskoye, 84
    Ukraine, xxxii, 74, 78
    Ural(s) Mountains, 84
    Wjasma, *141*
Red Army, 84, 97
    Red Army weapons/equipment
        BA 40 armored vehicle, *xlii*
        Ford Model A, 85
        Katuysha "Stalin organs" rockets, 25,
          82
        Polikarpov I 153 fighter aircraft, *73*
        Tupelov SB-2 bomber aircraft, *72*
        T-34/76 42 tank, *44*, *81*, 84
Soviet Union (USSR)/Russia
    country, *xviii*, *xxix*, xxx, xxxi, xxxii, xxxvi,
        xxxvii, 2, 5, 10, 11, 13, 15, 29, 31,

        35, 46, 60, 69, 78, 82, 85, 86, 88,
        92, 100, 108, 110, 112, 120, 123,
        125, 129, 132
    in photographs, *xvi*, *xxviii*, *xxvix*, *14, 16,
        28, 31, 36, 70–76, 79, 81, 82, 90,
        93, 94, 96, 97, 126, 127, 130, 139,
        140*
Soviet(s)/Russian(s)
    forces, *xvi*, *xxviii*, xxxii, 11, *44*, 51, *72*,
        74, 75, 78, *81*, 84–87, 95, 144
    partisan(s), *xix, 70*, 129
    soldiers, *26, 27*, 69, *71*, 74, 92
    winter ("General Winter"), 85–88, *89,
        90,* 91, *94*
    Winterschlacht Im Osten, 1941–42
        (Winter Campaign in the East), *38*
    Zhukov, Georgi, 95
SS. See German Government and Politics
Stalin, Joseph (USSR), 82, 94, 136, 138
Strait of Messina, 106
Sutner, Maria, 1
Switzerland, 22, 144

U

United States, 120, 121, 132, 138
    as enemy, xvii, xxxi, 5, 128
U.S. Army, xiv, xxii, 29, 85
    Fifth Army, 108, 109
    Seventh Army, 106
    Tenth (X) Corps, 108
    Eleventh (XI) Corps, 108
    OSS (Office of Strategic Services), 22
    Persons
        Clark, Mark, 108
        Eisenhower, Dwight D., 109
        Patton, George S., 106
U.S. Marines, 125
U.S. Navy, xix

V

Vatican, xix, 119
Versailles, Treaty of, xxx
Vienna (Wien), Austria, xv, xxv, 1, *3*, 4, 10,
    12, 19, 21, 37, 64, 103, 117, 120,
    136, 143–46
Vienna *Kaserne*, 10
Vietnam War, 17, 129, 132
    Calley, William, 129
    My Lai, 129
Virginia, xiv, xv, 22, 145, 146
    Alexandria, xiv, 146
    Fort Belvoir, xv
Virginia Tech, Blacksburg, Va., 145

W

Warsaw, Poland, 46

Washington, D.C., 145
Wehrmacht (German Armed Forces), xv, xvii, xxi, xxx, xxxi, xxxiii, 4, 46, 47, 88
Frisch's friends
  Fallmann, Walter, *64*
  Filipsky, Karl, 117, *133*
  Kitchelt, Lothar, *102*
  Koptic, Karl, *4*
  Mahr, Franzi, 103
  Pendel, August "Gustel," *102*
  Penold, Gustav, 64
General Staff, 69, 111
German Army *(Heer)*, xiv, xv, xxi, xxii, xxxiii, xxxv, *xliii*, 5, 8, 13, 15, 17, 19, 22, 23, 35, 37, 53, *63*, 84, 88, *91*, 103, 104, 109, 112, 125
German common soldier(s), xxi
German soldier(s) *(soldat[en])*, xiv, xxi, xxii, xxxii, *xxxvi, 2, 9, 12*, 17, *18, 19*, 22, *28*, 35, 37, *39, 43*, 46, *50*
Kriegsmarine (Navy), xxxiii
Luftwaffe (Air Force), xxxiii
OKH (*Oberkommando des Heeres*, Army Command), xxxiii, xxxiv, xxxvi, 85
OKW (*Oberkommando der Wehrmacht, Wehrmacht* High Command), xxxiii, 60
Wehrmacht Awards
  Kriegsverdienstkreuz (*Winterorder*, "frozen meat medal") *(Gefrierfleischorden)*, 37, *38*
  Ritterkreuz, 15
Wehrmacht Forces (Field Units), 11
  Fourth Army, 35, 46, 73
  Sixth Army, 11
  Tenth Army, 22, 108
  Afrika Korps (Rommel's Africa Corps), 11, 15, 17, 100, 103
  Army Groups
    A, 51
    Center, 35, 73, 74, 78, 82
    South, 78
    Southwest, 110
  Artillerie (Artillery)
    Abteilung (Battalion) 557, xxi, xxxvii, 100, *109*
    1st Battery, xxi, *102*, 103, *105*
    2nd Battery, xxi, 103, 104
    3rd Battery, 103, 104, *109*
    Abteilung (Battalion) 109, 11, 100
    Regiment 109, *xviii*, xxxvii, 4, 10, 12, *14*, 17, 32, 46, *67*, 73, 95, *115*, 103
    1st Battalion, 10, 32
    1st Battery, 10
  Gross Deutschland, 100

IDF, 141
Panzer Units
  1st *Panzer* Division, 10
  3rd *Panzer* Army, 86
  4th *Panzer* Army, 86
  2nd *Panzer* Group (Guderian's), 73
  3rd *Panzer* Group, 73
  4th *Panzer* Group *(Panzergruppe)*, 73, 84
  XIX *Panzer* Corps, xxxiv, 46
  Guderian's *Panzer* Corps, xxxiv, 10, 56, 58
  Panzer Grenadier, xxxiii
  Pioniere, 49
  Volksgrenadier, xxxiii
  Volkssturm, xxxiii, xxxvi
Wehrmacht Leaders
  Bock, Fedor von, 73, 84
  Gehlen, Reinhard, 82
  Goering, Herman, 19
  Guderian, Heinz, xix, xxxiv, 10, 56, 58, 73, 85
  Halder, Franz, 85
  Heydrich, Reinhard, 32
  Hoeppner, Erich, 73, 84
  Hoth, Herman, 73, 74
  Jodl, Alfred, xxxiii
  Keitel, Wilhelm, xxxiii
  Kesselring, Albert, 22, 110
  Kirchner, General, 56
  Kleist, Ewald von, 56
  Kluge, Gunter Hans von, 73, 74
  List, Wilhelm, 56
  Rauss, Erhard, 86
  Rundstedt, Gerd von, 51
  Vietinghoff, Heinrich, 22, 108, 110, 112
  Wolff, Karl, 22, 110–12
Wehrmacht Weapons/Equipment
  88mm *Flak* gun, *34*
  15cm *Kanone* 18 (15cm K 18), xxxvii
  15cm *schwere Feldhaubitze* 18 (15cm S FH 18 [*Immergrun*]), xxxvii
  Horch KFZ 15 staff car, *63*
  Krausmaffai half-track vehicle, xxxvii, 11, *14*
  Mauser rifle, 35
  NSU motorcycle, *23*, 78
  P-38 pistol, 35
  Panzer Mark II PzKpfWII tank, *128*
  Steyr staff car, 11, *13, 57, 67*
  Sturmgeschuetz G III armored vehicle, *55, 77*
  10cm *Kanone* 18 (S 10cm K 18 [*Bleiganz*]), xxxvii, *23, 36, 82*
  Wanderer-Audi staff car, *25*
Wehrmachtsbericht, 24, 77
Werfel, Franz, 1

West, The, 144
West Germany, 128, 144
Western world, 94
Wilmington, N.C., xxi
World War I, xxx, xxxi, 5, *53*, 136, *142*
  Italian Front, 8
  Vladivostok, 8
World War II, xiv, xv, xxii, xxx, xxxvi, 5, 46,
      85, 129, 131
World War II magazine, xxi

Y

Yugoslavia, 13